A Handy Reference Guide

Without saying a word, your hands speak volumes about your personality. For example, the shape and size of your hands can help you gain insight into your strengths and weaknesses.

Do you have a long palm with long, slender fingers? If so, you have a water hand, which means you are a sensitive, sympathetic, and intuitive person who probably relies on emotions to make decisions. You may have to be careful of being overly self-critical.

Do you have a short palm with short fingers? Then you've got an earth hand, and you are practical, reliable, and productive, although you may have to watch out for becoming too single-minded or authoritarian.

Palmistry is also fun—in any social gathering, mention that you read palms and you'll soon have a crowd of people eager to find out more about themselves.

Palmistry: Quick & Easy is just that—quick and easy. With its detailed question-and-answer format, you'll gain a deeper understanding of yourself and the people around you—just by listening to what their hands have to say.

About the Author

Peter Hazel began reading palms in a Gypsy tea room in Townsville, far North Queensland, Australia. A professional palm reader, he has taught medical palmistry at the South Australian College of Botanic Medicine and Natural Therapies, and palmistry at the Adelaide College of Botanical Medicine. Palaeontology, cartomancy, and watercolor painting are among his other interests. This book is the basic text for his course. Other books by Peter Hazel include *The Compleat Dice Oracles* (Handmade Books Adelaide, 2001); *The Gypsy Dice Oracle* (Handmade Books Adelaide, 1994); and *Consulting the Coins—A New Interpretation of the I Ching* (Lothian Books, 1990).

To Write to the Author

If you wish to contact the author or would like more information about this book, please write to the author in care of Llewellyn Worldwide and we will forward your request. Both the author and publisher appreciate hearing from you and learning of your enjoyment of this book and how it has helped you. Llewellyn Worldwide cannot guarantee that every letter written to the author can be answered, but all will be forwarded. Please write to:

Peter Hazel
% Llewellyn Worldwide
P.O. Box 64383, Dept. 1-56718-410-3
St. Paul, MN 55164-0383, U.S.A.

Please enclose a self-addressed stamped envelope for reply, or $1.00 to cover costs. If outside U.S.A., enclose international postal reply coupon.

Many of Llewellyn's authors have websites with additional information and resources. For more information, please visit our website at http://www.llewellyn.com.

PALMISTRY

Quick & Easy

Peter Hazel

2001
Llewellyn Publications
St. Paul, Minnesota 55164-0383, U.S.A.

FIRST EDITION
First Printing, 2001

Book design by Donna Burch
Cover design and interior illustrations by Kevin R. Brown
Cover illustration © 2001 by Bonnie Belavitz

Library of Congress Cataloging-in-Publication Data

Hazel, Peter, 1947–
    Palmistry : quick & easy / Peter Hazel.— 1st ed.
        p. cm.
    Includes bibliographical references (p.) and index.
    ISBN 1-56718-410-3
        1. Palmistry. I. Title.

    BF921.H44 2001
    133.6—dc21   2001029938

Llewellyn Publications
A Division of Llewellyn Worldwide, Ltd.
P.O. Box 64383, Dept. 1-56718-410-3
St. Paul, MN 55164-0383, U.S.A.
www.llewellyn.com

Printed in the United States of America

Contents

Contents

Contents

Part Three: The Appendices

Palmistry has long been considered a mystic art, when in fact it is a valuable and precise method of qualifying and quantifying all aspects of human potential.

—Peter West

Lines have not been traced without cause in the hands of men. They evidently emanate from the influence of heaven and from human individuality.

—Aristotle

Preface

This book came into being during a period when, tempted by the vanity of teaching in the autumn of 1987, I taught a six-month course in medical palmistry at the South Australian College of Botanic Medicine and Natural Therapies. There was a class of twelve, several of whom were fourth-year students of naturopathy; the remainder were interested adults. They were a formidably bright group, hungry for knowledge and good information.

The main problem for me as a teacher was to supply the students with a suitable text. I wanted to present them with an organized body of knowledge in some easily accessible form. This proved impossible to find.

My own knowledge was acquired slowly. Having no teacher, I relied on books, beginning with Katherine St. Hill and Cheiro, both famous palmists around the turn of the century. These writers were very keen on gloomy, moralistic interpretations. They had a good grasp of the traditional stream of palmistry, but this was colored by the particular social mores and crude psychological knowledge of their day. It takes a keen student to wade through all the Victorian prose and the jumbled, poorly organized mass of detail.

The Victorians took good, robust, medieval folk palmistry and gave it a good, hearty tweak. They overlaid the basic principles of traditional palmistry with their own worldview. For some odd reason, many natural human attributes, especially sexuality, were regarded negatively. A strict religious atmosphere may also have had an influence. Some readings from old texts are extremely sexist and racist and rather disapproving in tone. So signs of exceptional vitality in an individual were seen as problems. This has been overcome; unfortunately, many modern books are simply rewrites of the many Victorian texts published. (Incidentally, the way to tell whether or not a palmistry book in your collection is a genuine piece of modern telling or a Victorian rehash is to look at the chapter on mounts. We have three mounts directly beneath the fingers; if your book asserts there are four, it's Victorian palmistry warmed up!)

Adhering strictly to traditional nomenclature, I sorted Victorian value judgements from the data, and proceeded to create New Age views (I think of the New Age as the current evolutionary stage of humankind, of sentience, during which we are becoming more motivated by spiritual concerns rather than by political, mercenary, and other ideologies; the "new" age is often a rediscovery of old knowledge, but psychology and other arts made great advances in the last century). Some definitions were arrived at only after lengthy discussion with students and other practitioners. The result is the book you now hold in your hands. *Palmistry: Quick & Easy* is a technical manual designed for ease of use, which will provide instant access to an ancient art for both the experienced palmist and the novice.

Introduction

Palmistry is based on the belief that each part of the body reflects the state, both physical and mental, of the entire organism. When one is ill, there are many obvious physical signals. Your hair, skin, and coloring are all affected. Your body is an ecosystem, and everything in it is related and connected to everything else. The palm and the iris, in particular, are special in that they reflect the state of the entire organism.

Consider your hand; with its twenty-seven fine bones and intricate network of sinew and muscle, it is the most complex biological tool ever evolved. Its versatility is astonishing. It can lay bricks, sew, make love, kill, and wriggle in all directions at once. Just imagine life without your hands—how difficult it would be to get along without them. We use them to communicate when we speak and when we are silent; we use them to carry guns and to change diapers. Aristotle called the hand "the organ of organs, the active agent of the passive powers of the entire system."

It would be hard to imagine how human civilization could have developed without hands to build it. The hand is so full of information that even a handshake will tell you a great deal about a person. The hands also form one pole of our intricate nervous system (the feet are the other pole). Between them, the feet and hands contain more than one third of the body's surface nerve receptors, and both are rich in reflex points.

The palm is crisscrossed with lines: three major lines—the life, head, and heart lines—plus a variety of minor lines that appear on the hands of all normal people. However, variations in length, thickness, color, and regularity are infinite. Each of us has a unique hand, different to anybody else's. This is due to the fact that the lines are caused by the differences and experiences that make us individual.

It would be impossible to estimate the age of palmistry. There exist fragments of literature on palmistry from the Aryan age, some 6,000 years ago. Ancient Vedic literature from India contains many volumes on the subject. So it would appear that palmistry has existed as an established art for a very long time. It probably took many generations of careful observation, passed down verbally, to bone palmistry to its current precise form. Folk knowledge, in which we can include herbalism, shamanism in all its varieties, and even astronomy, is highly refined, legitimate, and useful information. This knowledge was hard-won: we know some mushrooms are deadly probably because long ago someone died after eating them. Folk knowledge is not rigid, however: it is added to and expanded by succeeding generations as social values change, and information no longer relevant is discarded.

Palmistry was also practiced in Greece where, in 423 B.C., Anaxagoras remarked that palmistry was "a study worthy of an enquiring and educated mind." It remained a worthy study until the advent of the Dark Age in Europe (A.D. 476), a period when religious fanaticism was at a peak, with alert clergy and pious laymen forever on the lookout for heresy. The history of Christianity at this time is a story of the suppression of knowledge. Palmistry, along with Wicca, astronomy, and herbalism, was brutally suppressed and its practitioners condemned, with the consequence that the art moved underground. Further reference to palmistry is not found until 1440.

During this dark period, palmistry became the province of Gypsies, whose skills were not very profound—usually woven about cheerful fortunes that would ensure good tips.

There was something of a revival in the nineteenth century, when the new scientific age brought forth men who tried to put palmistry on a scientific footing. Foremost among these are the Frenchmen D'Arpigny and Desbarolles, who systematically studied the hand, creating classifications still used by some palmists today.

Regrettably, however, official recognition of the science of palmistry is as far off today as it ever was. Though there exists, as any doctor would agree, a huge number of mysteries regarding the human body and the way it functions, palmistry has been rejected by physicians and academics without much investigation.

This folk knowledge has survived despite all opposition, however, and interest in it blossoms today. Palmistry, like naturopathy, herbalism, and astrology, may one day be fully accepted, which will give us another tool to explore the exquisite mystery of being human. Additionally, palmistry has the potential to become a major diagnostic tool for any profession that deals directly with people, like physicians, psychologists, and teachers.

That the palm is a mirror of the human self is a gift of nature. This book is a small contribution to the acceptance of palmistry as a legitimate discipline.

How to Use This Book

This portable palmistry workshop is designed to provide instant access to an ancient art. It consists of three parts: the Notes, the Workshop, and the Appendices.

The Notes provide vital information necessary for the serious student of palmistry, as well as for the interested layperson. They tell you what to look for on the lines and the mounts, and how to judge time, as well as other useful information.

The Workshop consists of a series of questions and answers that will take you methodically through a palm reading. To conduct a reading—of your own hand, or of a willing subject—simply work your way through the Workshop.

Each question requires a yes or a no answer. When the answer is yes, the accompanying description applies to the subject. If the answer is no, simply pass on to the next question.

These questions systematically examine the various aspects of the hand, beginning with broad outlines and continuing to explore the finer details, covering the lines and mounts and the marks on the fingers. Much of the material has come from original research, and has not appeared in print before.

You may complete the reading having received only a few or a great many yes answers. This reflects the simplicity or complexity of the subject. You may find contradictions; these can often represent conflict and contradiction within the subject.

Do not take any single definition as final. The golden rule of palmistry states that no one aspect should be considered in isolation. It is your task to weave the various definitions into a holistic picture of the subject (see Notes on interpretation and intuition).

Always read the right hand (see Notes on left and right hands).

Your first few readings may seem slow, even difficult, but regular use of this portable palmistry workshop will lead to familiarity and expertise.

Part One
The Notes

The ancient art and science of palmistry—the original and still the most accurate form of psychoanalysis—is not a quick study. The science of palmistry consists of being able to recognize and name the various lines, mounts, and signs. This exercises the left-hand side of the brain, the linear self. The art of palmistry consists of the interpretation of these same physical signs and how they complement each other, and this engages the right-hand side of the brain, the lateral self. To develop skill in palmistry, you need both the scientific perspective of empirical observation as well as the intuitive and artistic abilities to weave the signs into an accurate reading.

The Notes contain essential information that supplement and enhance the Workshop. There is a formidable mass of detail to be absorbed; however, a careful reading of the Notes, combined with use of the Workshop, will remove most of the difficulties usually associated with the study of palmistry.

Interpretation and Intuition

As you work your way through the Workshop, you may finish with only a few yes answers, or a great many. Since each definition contains a statement about a characteristic, representing a single facet of a personality, the number of yes answers reflects how complex and multifaceted the subject is.

Some of the answers will be contradictory, while others will complement and tend to confirm traits. Contradictory answers reflect conflict and contradiction in the subject. Most of us are a collection of traits, habits, and characteristics mixed with conditioning that somehow all balance out to form our individual personalities.

It is important that you, as the palmist, take a holistic view of the subject's personality. Yes answers should never be considered in isolation, nor should too much weight be given to a single aspect. This is the golden rule of palmistry: marks and signs must be seen as a part of a functioning whole. Negative indications are often modified by more positive signs elsewhere on the hand.

The objective is to look at the subject as a whole; to view the mass of information and to weigh it all up and see how it combines to make the subject the person he or she is.

Referral to the palmistic map of a person is a simple and nonthreatening procedure, full of interest for the subject of the reading and the reader. Just watch the reaction of your friends when you admit you are studying palmistry. Even the skeptics want a turn!

The hand displays a wealth of information. The art is to weave this information into a clear portrait—this is where intuition comes in.

Intuition

Intuition constitutes the inexact segment of the science and art of palmistry. Some of you will be gifted with intuition; others will, with practice, develop it. The information that feeds intuition comes from many sources: directly from the palm—for while you hold a subject's hand many subtle, unconscious impressions will be received—and the age, gender, clothing, and body language of the subject will also convey clues. Your own life experience and knowledge will also contribute to your intuition about a particular subject.

It is important for the serious student to read as many palms as they possibly can. Intuition is a muscle that strengthens with regular exercise.

Eventually, accuracy and confidence will grow, as will knowledge, and the need to refer to the text will decrease.

Don't be afraid of making mistakes. Have confidence in the basic accuracy of palmistry. If a subject denies some aspect of themselves that is clearly marked on their hand, it is more often than not a measure of that subject's lack of self-knowledge.

Methodology

Left and Right Hands

There are a variety of opinions concerning which hand should be read: "The future is shown in the right, the past in the left" is one such opinion. "Length of days is in her right hand, riches and honor are in her left" is a quotation from the Bible (Proverbs 3:16). However, it is more usual to read the right hand. Custom has it that potential shows in the left hand, while the right hand shows the realized personality. If the subject is left-handed, it is still usual to read the right hand, though (confusingly) sometimes the hands are reversed and the left is the right, so to speak. Only experience and instinct will tell you when you have to read the left as you would the right, and vice versa.

Another saying goes that the left hand is the one we are born with, and the right is what we have made of it.

And another has it that the right hand is read for men, while the left is read for women. Helped by relatively recent developments in psychology, modern palmistry has been able to clarify and enhance more traditional readings.

The Significance of the Left Hand

The left hand is controlled by the right brain, which regulates pattern recognition and understands the relationship between one thing and another. The left hand reflects the inner person. It is the yin aspect of the personality—the feminine, receptive side of the self. It is the natural self, with an aptitude for art. It is the anima—highly personal, intuitive, and erotic. And it is lateral thinking.

The left may be considered as a record of an individual's personal and spiritual development.

The Significance of the Right Hand

The right hand is controlled by the left brain, which regulates logic, reason, and language, and understands detail and how things work. The right hand reflects the outer person. It is the yang aspect of the personality—the masculine, active side of the self. It is the objective self and shows the influence of social environment, education, and experience. It is concerned with practical, outward matters, such as adaptation to society and the need to make a living. And it is linear thinking.

The right hand may be seen as the individual's adaptation to the environment, and the influence of family and society.

Compare

It is always worthwhile to study a subject's hands together, taking care to note down any major differences between the left and right. The ideal would be to have left and right hands identical. The subject in such a case would prove a very balanced and integrated person, with an inner self matched to the outer personality. This is fairly rare, however.

Hands can vary remarkably in shape, size, coloring, and, of course, in the major lines. These display the difference between the potential and the actual in a subject. The need to make a living and to conform often overpowers a creative talent, for instance. You are bound to find many people who have been altered by the realities of social pressures.

It is sobering to note that the left hand is often clearer and cleaner than the right, illustrating the degree of repression of the natural, intuitive, and erotic self by our society.

In the course of practice, I have come across notable exceptions to the "read the right hand" rule. These exceptions have been the lateral thinkers, the people whose right brains are dominant. In their cases, it was correct to read the left hand.

Experience is the only way you will learn to make fine distinctions. In the meanwhile, concentrate on the right hand, regarding the left as the potential.

Reading the Lines

Lines read literally, and should be examined for irregularities of any sort. It is useful to consider the lines as power cables on a grid. Very pale, faded lines are not very effective at carrying power. Thick, bright red lines may be all too efficient at energy-bearing, making the subject overactive, hypertense, or even violent. For examples of some of the irregularities found on lines, see Figure 1.

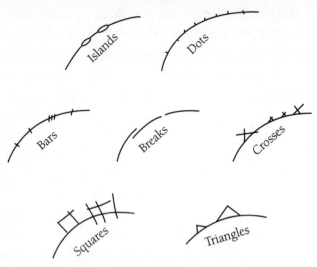

Figure 1: *Examples of irregularities on lines*

Islands

Islands are generally a negative sign and represent split energy. They usually signify a difficult period, often of change.

As the life line represents the physical self, an island here often represents a period of ill health. It can also show divided energy—perhaps someone who dislikes their work or their marriage.

An island on the head line may, among other things, represent mental trauma, at times as simple as disliking one's workplace to psychological problems, mild and severe. It can also be a record of an actual injury to the head. In addition, it may indicate divided intellectual loyalties—perhaps the person is leading a way of life not fully accepted.

On the heart line, it can mean divided emotional loyalties, hence the traditional interpretation of fickleness. It may also, accompanied by other signs in the hand, indicate cardiac disease.

Dots

Dots are full stops, and indicate a distinct interruption to the flow of energy. They are traditionally considered to be a sign of crisis. They certainly represent significant events.

On the life line, dots mean a major shakeup: retrenchment, failure, demotion, and so on. On the head line, they represent intellectual crisis. On the heart line, the crisis is emotional.

Bars

Bars are blockages and often represent influences that arise outside the personality.

On the life line, these are physical events—perhaps an actual barrier that must be faced and overcome.

On the head line, they are a sign of mental blocks that reflect worry or lack of concentration.

On the heart line, they may represent problems that arise within relationships, such as rejection and disillusionment.

Breaks

Breaks are exactly that: a sign that a serious and major change to one's routine is at work; of energy quitting the old way and taking a new path. This new path may be negative or positive, and this may be assessed by examining the quality of the line that continues after the break.

On the life line, breaks show travel, change of job, or divorce. On the head line they represent a complete change in thinking, opinion, or attitude.

On the heart line they are an indication of a clear break in affection (a broken heart), emotional disillusionment or disappointment, and rejection.

Crosses

Crosses on lines, fortunately rare, have long been considered to be negative signs. They often represent challenges to the subject: hurdles to be overcome, problems that beset everyday life.

The palmist should never forget that there are three common crosses that are fortunate, depending on location (see Crosses, pp. 12–13). Even simply knowing about difficult character traits can help people spur their growth.

Squares

Squares are a sign of protection and good fortune wherever they are found. They represent some environmental or personal factor that assists or protects the subject in most situations.

Triangles

Triangles are positive marks. They indicate talent, creative ability, and energy, and enhance the qualities of any line or mount on which they appear.

Stars

These are fairly uncommon signs that may indicate brilliance in a positive, well-formed character. In a negative hand, they may indicate disaster, either enhancing or disrupting whatever line or mount on which they appear.

When studying the lines, do not be afraid to ask the subject questions about their past. A little judicious questioning can clarify and assist your reading a great deal. You will always run up against the character who will answer your questions with "You're the palmist, you tell me." My suggested reply to this is: "When your doctor asks where it hurts, do you reply, 'Well, you're the doctor, you tell me'?"

Above all, don't be afraid of making mistakes!

Reading the Mounts

Novices often find the mounts difficult to locate and to access. It may help to consider the mounts as zones or areas on the palm, rather than look for bumps. Proper and accurate judgment of their size will only come with patience and experience.

There are several marks that commonly appear on the mounts (see Figure 2). For mount location, see pp. 141–164.

Verticals

Verticals are signs of vitality and energy in whatever area they are found.

Horizontals

Horizontals are marks indicating stress, frustration, and other problems wherever they are found. They can also represent disruptive influences. For example, on mount six (Venus), horizontals can show the interference and influence of close family and friends.

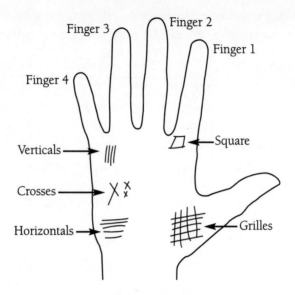

Figure 2: Common marks on the mounts

Crosses

Crosses are usually considered negative signs, but there are at least three cases when crosses are a positive indication:

1: The happy marriage cross, which lies in the area directly below finger one, shows a personal disposition toward, and a talent for, fostering and nurturing relationships. Its absence, however, does not indicate the opposite.

2: The mystic cross, which is located between the head and heart lines, in the area beneath fingers two and three. According to tradition, it indicates an interest in and a talent for occult (alternative) science.

3: The battle cross, which lies between the fate and life lines toward the base of the palm. Some traditions claim it means that the subject will save a life (or has already done so), while others say it shows a very quarrelsome disposition, with a love of battle. You may make up your own mind about this cross.

Elsewhere, crosses represent trouble and worry, disappointment and unfavorable change. Here is a brief list of traditional readings:

Under finger two: A sign of an accident-prone personality; a gloomy pessimist.

Under finger three: Signals the frustrated artist; failure to translate artistic talent into material form.

Under finger four: Indicates dishonesty, exaggeration, lying, and scheming.

On mount four (Mars positive): Marks a violent nature that resorts to force as a matter of policy.

On mount eight (Moon): Shows a defect in imagination, or an overactive imagination leading to daydreaming, possible paranoia, and withdrawal into a fantasy world; a person isolated from reality.

On mount six (Venus): Some traditions say it indicates an all-consuming love, others that it signals an unhappy marriage or love affair, or family in-fighting. Once again, you may make your own judgment.

Generally, crosses may be interpreted as disruptions to the coping process. They usually reflect a sensitive and delicate personality with a tendency to transform small and trivial issues into large problems.

Grilles

Grilles show a scrambling of energy. They signal some form of malfunction where they occur, transforming the energy of the area so that, for example, ambition becomes unhealthy obsession, love becomes selfish sensuality, executive skill becomes bullying, and so on. It often represents confusion because the energy of the mount involved becomes scattered and undirected.

Squares

These are positive signs of protection and preservation wherever they are found.

Time

Measurement of Time on the Major Lines

When considered as a diagnostic and psychoanalytic tool, the hand is unique as it includes the fourth dimension of time.

While the palm and the lines render the history of the subject accurately, the future is yet unformed, and consists of probabilities and possibilities. A competent palmist can read these probabilities, but it should be clearly understood that any predictions are only possibilities. Remember, also, that lines can change. If a hand shows distinct signs of fu-

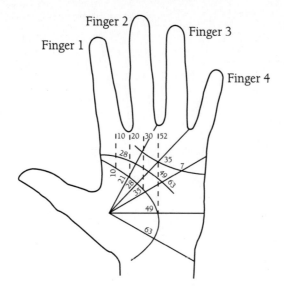

Figure 3: Ways to judge time

ture degeneration due to drug use or lifestyle, it is not necessarily an inevitable outcome. If a person changes his or her habits, the lines will change accordingly, reflecting the new future that will result. (See Notes on predicting the future on page 21.)

There are several ways to judge time on a line. Again, you will find that accuracy comes with practice.

Cheiro, a Victorian palmist, divided the major lines into ten equal parts and assigned seven years to each division. Here are two other useful methods I have found to be a fairly accurate guide (see Figure 3).

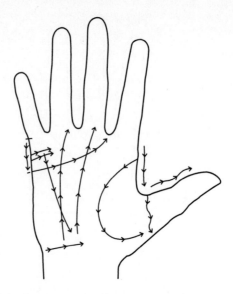

Figure 4: The direction of time flow on the major lines

1: In Figure 3, you will see dashed, straight lines drawn downward from the bases of the fingers until they intersect the life line.

A straight line drawn down from the middle of finger one will intersect the life line at ten years of age. A straight line drawn down from between fingers one and two will intersect the life line at age twenty. A line from the middle of finger two will cross the life line at age thirty-five. After that, the life line curves away. These readings are only generally accurate, with an error factor of plus or minus a year.

2: Simply measure the line in question and divide it in half, then into quarters. If you judge the average life span to be seventy-five years, the halfway mark must be thirty-seven or thirty-eight, and the quarters will mark the nineteenth and fifty-sixth years. You could then halve the quarters, giving you the tenth, twenty-eighth, forty-seventh, and sixty-sixth years.

You must take care to read the time flow for each line in the right direction. Figure 4 shows the direction of time flow on the major lines.

Rings

There are some things you can observe before examining a subject's palm that will reveal a great deal about his or her character. This section is included because sometimes rings people wear can reveal some aspects of character.

The ring ought to be seen literally, i.e., the quality of the ring. It should be emphasized that these readings of personal choice in jewelry are rather judgmental and negative, reflecting Victorian values.

Modern palmists tend to see rings in two perspectives: as a one-word description (rich, tasteful, expressive, ostentatious, etc.) and as an emphasis of the qualities of the finger involved. But good palmists should always remember that, sometimes, a ring is just a ring! Otherwise, the negative, traditional readings should be seen as challenges for subjects to be more balanced.

All this is based, of course, on the idea that adoring oneself is somehow "vanity" and therefore bad. However, in a good, well-formed hand, the ring is a positive sign relating to the qualities of the finger.

Rings (except for those worn on the third finger of the left hand, i.e., wedding rings) may be considered an indication of difficulties within a person. The wearing of a ring tends to cut off the qualities of the finger on which it is worn. The actual size of the rings may also be significant. Small, unobtrusive rings signify a lesser influence than large, ornate rings.

The following is a brief list of the traditional meanings of the fingers.

Right Hand

Finger One

If the finger is short, this person is troubled by an inferiority complex, and may overcompensate for the perceived lack by becoming a dominating, bullying tyrant.

If the finger is long, the person may be a chronic complainer who is never satisfied.

Finger Two

If the finger is short, this person is unstable and lacks self-discipline.

If the finger is long, the person is a critical, nagging complainer; a holier-than-thou troublemaker.

Finger Three

Whether short or long, the subject is experiencing frustration in their artistic or creative impulses; these may be caused by emotional ties, or a failure to create or exploit opportunities.

Finger Four

If short or long, the traditional reading is of dishonesty in business, or difficulties with relationships and sexual matters.

The Thumb
Indicates one who is dissatisfied with sex in general, or with their current relationships.

Left Hand

Finger One
If the finger is short, this is a sign of an inferiority complex compensated for by internal excess, overachievement, and overindulgence in food, sex, and alcohol.

If the finger is long, this may be a person with a superiority complex who is troubled by their feelings and takes refuge in false modesty and self-depreciation.

Finger Two
If short, the lack of self-discipline within this person will be disguised yet visible through unreliability and instability.

If long, this may be a repressed, guilt-ridden person who suffers from inner turmoil and lack of self-respect.

Finger Three
Whether short or long, the wearing of more than one ring (e.g., a wedding band plus engagement, eternity, or friendship rings) indicates emotional difficulties and problems in marriage or relationships.

Finger Four
Whether short or long, a ring here is a sign of sexual and relationship problems, possibly inherited from the parents.

The Thumb
A sign of a person who experiences problems with sexual acts, and who may be frigid or impotent.

Using the Readings

Predicting the Future

It is unwise to try to predict the future. Despite claims to the contrary, people persist in believing in predictions, and the danger of the self-fulfilling prophecy is always present.

Just announce at any party or social gathering that you read palms, and watch the people line up for their readings. Even skeptics seldom forget what you tell them.

Unfortunately, the type of palmistry that comes to the mind of most people is of the gypsy-in-a-tea-room variety, wherein the hand is scanned briefly and is followed by an enigmatic pronouncement concerning the past and future. A stock of phrases general enough to be true for most people is used.

Palmistry deals with the person as they are at the time of the reading. Of course, the palm being a map of time as well as other dimensions, it is possible to see past and future possibilities, probabilities, and likelihoods. It is not possible, however, to predict accidents and disappointments or lotto wins. These things, should they occur, will appear in the hand. One's history is traced with accuracy in the palm, but the future doesn't exist.

The fact is, the palm itself changes a great deal. Lines can appear and disappear overnight. What is on the palm doesn't change the person; rather, as people change, so do their palms.

Nevertheless, you will find that people generally believe that palmists are arcane mystics who can see into the future. Many people patronize palmists for that very reason.

However, the proper role of the palmist is to teach people about themselves, to give a gift of self-knowledge. In all likelihood the palmist will discern probabilities and trends regarding the personality and health of a subject in the course of a reading, but it should always be stressed these are just possibilities, not inevitabilities, and that negative indications can be averted by taking appropriate steps.

Reading Your Own Hand

The Workshop is a biofeedback device. Just sit down and answer each question as honestly as you are able. (This can be more difficult than it sounds!) You may well find yourself disagreeing with some of the answers. These are possibly aspects of yourself that you either do not recognize or do not wish to face up to; as such, these are the areas that require the most attention.

In any case, the Workshop offers you a unique opportunity for self-knowledge.

Naming the Demons

Each of us is a mixture of conflicting and complementary traits. If you have ever been puzzled by your own behavior, or confused by your emotions, the Workshop can go a long way toward explaining and clarifying the way your intellectual and emotional energies work.

The fairy tale of Rumpelstiltskin will be familiar to many. Briefly, it describes how a young girl defeats a supernatural being (i.e., a subconscious aspect of herself) by discovering his name. The power of names is a common theme in mythology.

Now you too have the means to name your own personal demons, and it is astonishing just how much understanding, sympathy, and even love for ourselves we can achieve simply by becoming self-aware, by tapping directly into the deep well of our feelings and behavior.

Your exploration of yourself can also reveal hidden or undeveloped talents, faults and limitations. This is the basis of self-knowledge. You can't change what you are not aware of.

So, name your demons, while not forgetting to celebrate and exploit your positive qualities. Remember, also, that your hand changes over time, and so it is possible to monitor yourself over a long period as lines change, appear, and disappear, recording advances and changes in your makeup that result from experience.

The study of palmistry will in itself modify your hand as you add to your store of understanding of what Dr. Johnson called "the greatest study of mankind"—which is, of course, people.

Part Two
The Workshop

The Workshop is designed to lead the novice through a reading. It consists of over 300 questions with answers that will cover most aspects of a reading.

Each question requires a yes or a no answer. If the answer is yes, the accompanying definition applies to the subject. If the answer is no, simply pass on to the next question.

As you become familiar with this system, your need to refer to it will decrease. Laid out according to traditional classifications, e.g., in lines and mounts, it is an easy-to-use reference.

The Hand

The hand shows the broad outlines of a person's character. The first step is to ascertain the hand type. There are four main types. To do this, measure the palm, which is the space between the base of the fingers and the wrist creases (bracelets), and determine whether it is short or long.

Figure 5: Measuring the palm

A *short* palm is square, or wider than it is long.

A *long* palm is longer than it is wide.

Now determine whether the fingers are short or long. To do this, measure the palm and fingers as shown in the figures.

Short fingers are equal to or shorter than the palm.

Long fingers are longer than the palm.

Has the hand . . .

A long palm with long fingers (water hand)?
This is also called the sensitive hand. It is the hand of a sensitive, sympathetic, cautious, reserved, intuitive, and

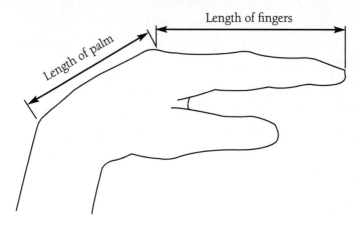

Figure 6: Measuring the fingers

psychic person with emotion-based reasoning and a rich inner life. Concern for taste and appearance and quality of lifestyle and relationships are characteristic of this personality, as is a caring nature and a sense of justice.

These people tend toward procrastination and may be overly self-critical, however. In need of constant encouragement and support, they may lack confidence, wilting easily in the face of criticism and opposition.

Love life: Sentimental and romantic, the water hand is easily ruled by love, and needs harmony and safe, comfortable surroundings.

A long palm with short fingers (fire hand)?

This is also called the instinctive hand. It signals an artistic, changeable, passionate, and creative personality—an adventurous risk-taker. These people are nonauthoritarian, highly motivated, extroverted, emotional, excitable, and prone to sudden enthusiasm. They may be overly emotional, and can be selfish, aggressive, and demanding.

Love life: Impulsive and easily bored by routine, fire hands need intensity and variety, and are usually sentimental and romantic.

A short palm with long fingers (air hand)?

This is known as the intellectual hand. It is the sign of a clever, interested personality, with a curious mind and a love of study. This person is intellectual in outlook, very analytical, systematic, and conceptualizing, and in possession of good communications skills. Reason tends to rule the emotions of such people, who may fear the irrational pressures of emotions. They can be cool and unsympathetic, impatient with routine, restless, and feel the need to be fully interested in whatever they are doing.

Love life: A love of adventure and novelty and a dislike of routine relationships distinguish the air hand.

A short palm with short fingers (earth hand)?

This is also known as the practical hand. It is the hand of a practical, conventional, reliable personality; solid, strict, strong, and productive.

He or she is likely to be authoritarian in outlook, with a love of order, routine, and systems, and a dislike of uncertainty and change. Cautious and single-minded, the person with this shape of hand tends to need material security, and is prone to temper attacks when stressed.

Love life: A need for security and regularity dominates; earth hands are nonadventurous, preferring routine to change.

Now feel the subject's hand all over. Is the hand . . .

Very soft and spongy to the touch?

This denotes sensuality and self-interest—one who delights in eating, drinking, and sexual pleasure, but who may be prone to obesity and in danger of overindulgence, addiction, and dependency.

It also shows a dislike of drudgery, routine, discomfort, and privation. People with this type of hand are usually very friendly, generous, and gregarious.

Quite flexible—the fingers bend backward easily?

This indicates the flexible nature of one with many interests and hobbies, who may be multitalented. It is the sign of a versatile and adaptable person with good coping skills, who enjoys and seeks change and novelty.

However, restlessness and an inability to settle down may also be a trait of the person with this type of hand. This may give rise to the "jack-of-all-trades, master of none" type.

Hard, stiff, and unyielding?

This shows an unyielding personality, resolute and determined, who may be stubborn and finds it difficult to compromise. Poor diplomatic skills and tactlessness are also potential traits, along with fixed attitudes and difficulty in coping with change.

This hand often belongs to one who is active and physical.

Firm, yet quite elastic?

This is the mark of a balanced type, adaptable to changing life and work situations, with a positive, optimistic outlook.

Such people are self-reliant and usually able to enjoy life.

Very smooth?

This suggests a creative personality that is impulsive, versatile, and adaptable; one who may be poetic, romantic, and imaginative. In a badly aspected hand—i.e., a hand in which the indications tend toward negative interpretation—it can indicate dishonesty, exaggeration, and posing, and a lack of attention to detail.

Very bony or knobby?

This is sometimes called the philosophical hand and indicates the intellectual outlook of one given to reflection and a liking for order and systems.

The negative aspects of this feature are dogmatic viewpoints, fault-finding with anyone who does not agree, and tactlessness. The subject may also be prone to worry and tension.

Hard and thin?

This can be the hand of one with delicate health, i.e., chronic conditions. Psychologically, it can show a person who isn't emotionally passionate, and who may seem to be cool and uninvolved to others—a person who appears unsympathetic and basically motivated by self-interest.

Distinctly hollow in the middle of the palm?

This points to a shy, timid person who has self-confidence issues to confront. Generally, it's a sign of poor self-esteem and a lack of self-confidence—something that can be worked on.

The subject with this feature may be prone to worry and pessimism, and possibly lacks self-knowledge.

Note the coloring. Is the hand . . .

Pale, colorless?

This is a rare sign. It can indicate poor health, with a general lack of physical energy. Psychologically, this is a very reserved person, who appears to others to be a withdrawn, egocentric person.

Pinkish, possibly mottled with white?

This is the normal color of basic good health, and shows a tendency to buoyant animal spirits.

Red, or with large red patches?

This shows vitality and high energy, vigor and sensuality. If very red, it is a sign of a tendency toward aggression and violence. In women, it is a possible indication of pregnancy or a hormone imbalance.

Compare the hand size to the overall physique of the subject. Are the hands . . .

Proportionally large?

This signals a talent for detail and minutiae, with a capability for fine and delicate work, possibly in crafts and arts. These people enjoy detailed, drawn-out analysis of relationships and situations.

Proportionally small?

This is a sign of one who is capable of grasping ideas as a whole, though perhaps not in fine detail; a person who is likely to see the overview, but who finds it harder to come to grips with the components of a situation.

Small-handed people often make good managers. Sometimes an inability to judge one's personal limits can be an asset, though small-handed people have to be careful of becoming unrealistic dreamers. They are able to visualize large-scale plans and schemes. The main challenge for them is to learn how to pay attention to details.

Well-proportioned?

Well-proportioned hands that seem neither too large nor too small are well-balanced, showing a subject who is neither too bogged down in detail nor absorbed by the big picture. The majority of people have the "normal sized," well-proportioned hand.

Examine the number of lines visible in the palm. Is the palm . . .

Covered with many lines (full or crowded hand)?

This is called the full or crowded hand and often belongs to a highly strung individual with a vivid imagination who is perceptive and often oversensitive. The crowded hand can also indicate creativity, unpredictability, and excitability. These people are often good at organizing and delegating, but are themselves fairly impractical. They are disciplinarians, yet poor at self-discipline. The many lines actually represent an abundance of energy that may be scattered or

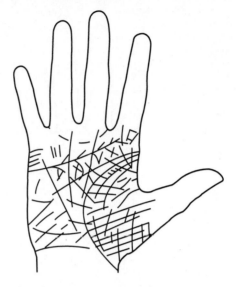

Figure 7: A full or crowded hand

poorly directed unless the subject is mindful and learns how to concentrate and use the energy (see Figure 7).

Marked with a moderate number of clear lines (moderate hand)?

This indicates a good balance between enthusiasm and indifference, with a tendency toward practicality (see Figure 8).

Marked with only a few basic lines (empty hand)?

The meaning of this varies with each hand type. In a sensitive water or fire hand, it can be a sign of deep spirituality, and the mark of a self-assured person. Indian palmistry calls it the mark of an old soul.

In more elementary hands (earth or air), it shows a no-nonsense, straightforward, unoriginal character; one well

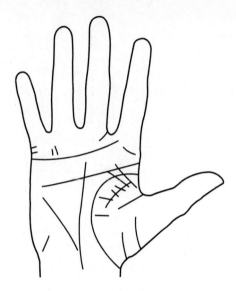

Figure 8: A moderate hand

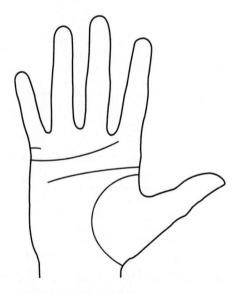

Figure 9: An empty hand

suited to service, who is conventional, obedient, punctual, and orderly. They work slowly, but are very thorough and meticulous (see Figure 9).

In relation to the palm, are the fingers . . .

Longer?
This denotes a sensitive, artistic nature, and a love of detail; possibly spiritually inclined, but with an element of pride that can lead to intolerance.

Shorter?
This shows a concise, precise person, quick to make judgment; one who can see things as a whole, but who may be troubled or intimidated by detail.

About equal in length?
Represents a balance between long and short fingers; honesty.

Now, examine the fingertips. Are they . . .

Round?
This is the ordinary shape and represents a strong-minded, intellectual person whose actions are based in both reason and emotion (see Figure 10).

Square?
A sign of practicality and craftsmanship, square fingertips indicate a physically strong person whose actions are based on reason (see Figure 11).

Figure 10: Round fingertip

Figure 11: Square fingertip

Figure 12: Spatulate fingertip

Figure 13: Pointed fingertip

Spatulate?

This shows a practical, capable person, who may be a good instigator and organizer (see Figure 12).

Pointed?

Indicates a person who acts mainly through intuition and emotion. These are traditionally described as psychic fingers (see Figure 13).

Does the little finger curve inward?

This is often called the wilt of self-sacrifice, indicating a self-effacing, compromising, compliant, anything-for-peace type of person. The self-sacrifice may make the subject appear a little masochistic, as they are usually so willing to please others they often tolerate selfish or demanding behavior in others. In a very well-aspected hand, it can represent business ability and financial skill (see Figure 14).

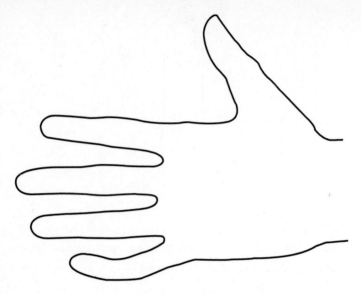

Figure 14: The wilt of self-sacrifice

The Thumb

The thumb represents the ego, and shows characteristics of self-confidence, stubbornness, logical ability, willpower, and determination.

First you must determine whether the subject has a long or short thumb. To do this, lay the thumb alongside the edge of the hand.

If the thumb reaches halfway along the bottom phalange of the index finger, it is *long*.

If it does not reach halfway along this phalange, it is *short*.

Is the thumb . . .

Long?

This shows a strong character with a developed sense of duty, intellectual strength, and an active ego. People with these thumbs tend to be ruled by emotion in a dogmatic way; they are very practical people, able to put ideas into action and transform dreams into reality. It also indicates ambition and strong will.

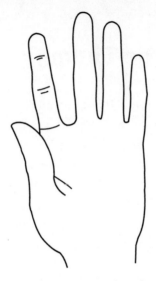

Figure 15: A medium thumb

Medium?

Most people have the medium thumb (see Figure 15). This is when the thumb appears to be neither large nor small in relation to the size of the hand. This is an indication of a person with "normal" powers of rational thought and will. They make decisions based on a balance between logical and emotional considerations.

Short?

An exceedingly rare occurrence, this indicates weak will, poor logical powers, and little ambition. People with these thumbs are generally ruled by emotional considerations, and are likely to have close family ties due to a sense of insecurity.

They are often indecisive, given to procrastination, and lack personal energy and power. They may also be bad-tempered, and capable of bursts of passionate, self-righteous anger.

Quite stiff, inflexible, and unyielding?
This signifies an inflexible, dogmatic, stubborn, and probably tactless individual with a rigid personality and poor coping skills. This person may well be self-absorbed and unable to see another's point of view.

This thumb is the mark of an unimaginative, unsympathetic character who must have his or her own way.

Rather supple and flexible?
This shows a charming, graceful character, very tactful, and a convincing flatterer. The flexible thumb indicates a very flexible ego, capable of compromise and sympathy to others' viewpoints.

People with this type of thumb are usually accommodating and cope with life skillfully.

Does it . . .

Curve backward at the tip?
Yes: This indicates a talent for living—one that is extravagant, adaptable, quick to learn, and often in possession of a contented nature. The person with this thumb has considerable willpower, modified by genuine concern for others, and is a skilled and convincing liar if the occasion demands.

No: This marks a very practical, stiff-necked, stubborn character, one that is terminally determined, yet usually very cautious, secretive, and self-controlled (see Figure 16).

Is the thumb . . .

Set low on the hand, near the wrist?
This suggests a creative, generous, and extravagant nature that is gregarious, sociable, hospitable, and outgoing.

It also shows an ego deeply rooted in emotion, of one who acts and reasons through feelings rather than logic (see Figure 17).

Set high on the hand, near the fingers?
This is the mark of a cautious, conservative nature with a tendency to be stubborn.

The person with this thumb has a very intellectual outlook, with most actions and relationships governed by logic rather than feeling (see Figure 18).

Now study the hand in a relaxed attitude, noting the angle that the thumb juts from the hand.

Is this angle . . .

Narrow (less than thirty degrees)?
Indicates an introvert who naturally has limited responses to others, and is not conventionally ambitious. Such persons are usually self-absorbed and may seem to others to be motivated mainly by self-interest.

Figure 16: A thumb that doesn't curve at the tip

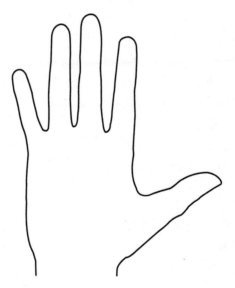

Figure 17: A low-set thumb

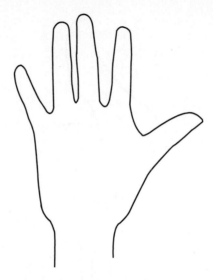

Figure 18: A high-set thumb

Wide (more than thirty degrees)?
The wider the angle, the more pronounced the characteristics of discipline, willpower, and sense of direction. This is a sign of an extrovert, one who is courageous and has leadership qualities.

Note the shape of the tip. Is it . . .
Pointed?
An intuitive, frivolous, and possibly superstitious person.

Square?
Shows a stubborn, practical, sagacious, and loyal person.

Round?
Indicates a balance between logic and emotion.

Clubbed?
The sign of a bad-tempered, violent nature. Fortunately a rare sign, the bulbous thumb has traditionally been called the murderer's thumb since medieval times.

Flat and thin?
People with subtle, quick minds, but low physical energy. Their challenge is to finish what they start.

Broad and thick?
A materialist; sensual, with a love of luxury.

Short and thick?
A rare mark, this indicates brutality, gross instincts, and low tastes. Can be a loyal minion, but makes a cruel tyrant.

Now, measure and compare the lengths of the first and the second phalanges of the thumb (see Figure 19).

Is the first phalange . . .

Shorter than the second?
Logic rather than ambition or blind willpower guides the person with this characteristic. They make emotionally reasoned decisions that are usually very logical, and possess tact, charm, and an ability to compromise (see Figure 20).

Longer than the second?
This signifies a predominance of willpower in the ego, one who is likely to be stubborn and unable to compromise. If very much longer, it can indicate a personality likely to conflict and disagree with others, an argumentative person

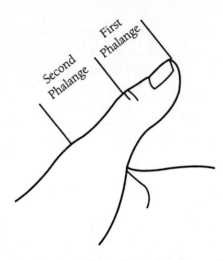

Figure 19: Comparing the first and second phalanges of the thumb

who must have his or her own way, and cannot be reasoned with (see Figure 21).

Are the two phalanges equal in length?

This is a sign of balance, where logic and will work together; it indicates a humane and sensitive person with good decision-making skills.

Is the thumb waisted, i.e., narrow in the middle of the second phalange when viewed frontally?

As the waist affects the so-called phalange of logic, the subject may often act through emotional impulse. Traditionally, it also gives the subject an ability to deal with people diplomatically (see Figure 22).

Figure 20: First phalange shorter than the second

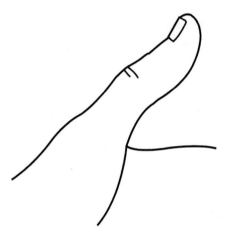

Figure 21: First phalange longer than the second

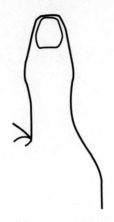

Figure 22: A waisted thumb

Marks on Fingers

The markings on the fingers show specific talents and problems in certain areas (see Figure 23). Because the phalanges relate to the twelve signs of the zodiac, these marks can be of particular use to astrologers.

There are four commonly occurring marks:

Vertical Lines
These are signs of positive energy. Astrologically, a good aspect.

Grilles
These are a mark of confused, undirected energy. Astrologically, grilles are possibly neutral.

Crosses
These signal misapplied or diverted energy. Astrologically, a bad aspect.

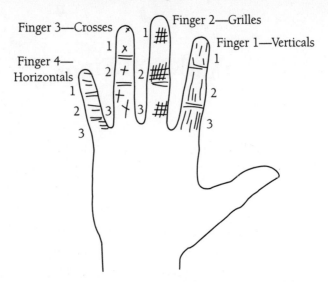

Figure 23: The most common marks

Horizontal Lines
These are stress marks and signal blocked energy. Astrologically, some form of retrograde activity is indicated.

Now, examine each finger, starting with the index, or Jupiter, finger. Begin at the tip and read down toward the palm. When any phalange has no marks at all, it is a sign of positive potential that is as yet unrealized. On all the first phalanges (fingertips), the fingerprints will be very noticeable (see the section on Fingerprints beginning on page 175).

Finger One, Phalange One
Does this phalange have . . .

Verticals?
A sign of inspirational spiritual skills, religious fervor, or leadership skills.

Grilles?
Incarceration, imprisonment, or seclusion of some sort, possibly in a monastery or in artistic isolation; one imprisoned by their beliefs.

Crosses?
Indicates absorption with religious or moral issues, which can place the subject out of step with society at large and the consensus reality.

Horizontals?
These are stress marks, indicating failure of religious aspirations, an inspiration block, or distraction of vital energy into trivialities.

Finger One, Phalange Two
Does this phalange have . . .

Verticals?
Signifies noble and idealistic ambitions; one motivated by morals and ethical ideals.

Grilles?
Self-deception; lack of self-knowledge.

Crosses?
A disposition to envy; one with a tendency to lie, misinform, plot, and manipulate others.

Horizontals?
Signs of stress, indicating that high ideals and ethics are not being lived up to.

Finger One, Phalange Three
Does this phalange have . . .

Verticals?
Strong executive drive, good organizational skills, plausibility.

Grilles?
Likelihood of abuse of personal power in personal and business life.

Crosses?
This sign indicates that sometimes a lack of appreciation for the feelings and needs of others can make this person seem exploitative and manipulative. Their challenge is to be more mindful.

Horizontals?
Stress due to frustration of, or lack of, ambition. Despite pressure to achieve, there is no strong desire to obtain power.

Finger Two, Phalange One
Does this phalange have . . .

Verticals?
The subject feels a strong sense of responsibility (be it personal or civic), a strong sense of duty, and need for material security.

Grilles?
Grilles usually indicate scrambled or confused energy. Such a sign indicates that the subject needs to be aware of the fact that perhaps they have been conditioned to fail.

Crosses?

Fortunately, a rare mark signalling a superstitious person who may be quite instinctive. There is a likelihood of anti-social tendencies, which possibly take the form of crimes to property.

Horizontals?

Stress due to the weight of responsibility, and perhaps a sense of failing in one's duty. This can also indicate being overworked.

Finger Two, Phalange Two
Does this phalange have . . .

Verticals?

A sign of academic ability and scientific interests; one interested in truth.

Grilles?

This mark shows the habitual pessimist, whose fatalistic attitude makes progress difficult and unlikely.

Crosses?

A mark of one with a cold and detached attitude based on a distorted view of reality. He or she may also be eccentric or bigoted.

Horizontals?

Stress caused by academic pressures. This can also indicate a turning away from consensus reality or taking refuge in cultivated ignorance.

Finger Two, Phalange Three
Does this phalange have . . .

Verticals?
A person with good common sense and financial abilities, with a love of security and comfort; often actively seeking self-development.

Grilles?
A person who may be confused with life, and is not usually capable of judging their own abilities and limitations. This may seem to others to be a lack of common sense.

Crosses?
A sign that the normal mental development of the subject has been sidetracked into unimportant or trivial paths.

Horizontals?
Stress caused by poor attitudes and behavior; a friendless or unlucky person, lacking common sense.

Finger Three, Phalange One
Does this phalange have . . .

Verticals?
Signifies an extreme form of sensitivity, possibly artistic genius; one with a high order of creative skills, originality, and energy.

Grilles?
A sign that sensitivity has scrambled to a painful intensity, provoking retreat, withdrawal, and depression.

Crosses?

Creativity has been diverted into trivial or antisocial ends.

Horizontals?

A sign of stress caused by some obstacle to the free and inspired expression of creative talent.

Finger Three, Phalange Two
Does this phalange have . . .

Verticals?

The sign of an outwardly expressive artist who is competitive, with a keen appreciation of commercial aspects.

Grilles?

The mark of an envious, frustrated artist who lacks insight and sensitivity.

Crosses?

Talent diverted into trivial ends.

Horizontals?

Stress caused by obstacles to the flow of artistic expression.

Finger Three, Phalange Three
Does this phalange have . . .

Verticals?

Analysis and perception; the mark of the artisan or craftsman who pays attention to detail and has a drive to achieve perfection.

Grilles?

A sign of perfection heightened to the point of obsession; a perfectionist.

Crosses?

Here is a need for personal perfection. No one is perfect, so this obsession is usually doomed to failure, in which case it leads to self-castigation.

Horizontals?

Stress; obstacles hampering the free flow of creative energy.

Finger Four, Phalange One
Does this phalange have . . .

Verticals?

A skilled communicator—eloquent, diplomatic, and tactful. This person has a love of harmony and luxury.

Grilles?

Communication skills may need training and refining.

Crosses?

A sign that communication skills are used for selfish motives.

Horizontals?

Stress caused by some hindrance to self-expression; a boaster.

Finger Four, Phalange Two
Does the phalange have . . .

Verticals?

A sign of potency and fertility, these indicate a person with developed sexual communication skills; a deep, sincere, and passionate person.

Grilles?
A sign of a person uncomfortable with deep emotional or sexual communication skills. These personal skills may need training and refining.

Crosses?
One whose sexual communication skills are used in a negative way; a person who is sexually aggressive, predatory, cunning, and selfish.

Horizontals?
Stress caused by problems in sexual communication. They can also indicate infertility or gynecological disorders.

Finger Four, Phalange Three
Does this phalange have . . .

Verticals?
An articulate and truthful communicator, with good salesmanship skills.

Grilles?
An unmindful communicator who is prone to speak first, then think later. May seem tactless at times.

Crosses?
One who may be prone to exaggeration and, at worst, to lying.

Horizontals?
Stress indicating inarticulate expression, leading to misunderstanding.

The Thumb, Phalange One
Does this phalange have . . .

Verticals?
A sign of a strong will, energy, confidence, and strength; one whose will is often obeyed.

Grilles?
A mark of scattered willpower—energy is diverted into trivial and unimportant matters.

Crosses?
A sign of unusual obstinacy, mindless stubbornness, and inability to compromise.

Horizontals?
These are stress marks, bars to the free expression of will, and show someone whose will may often be thwarted and who may lack confidence.

The Thumb, Phalange Two
Does the phalange have . . .

Verticals?
A sign of good powers of logic and reasoning, and common sense.

Grilles?
Flawed powers of reasoning; dishonesty; one who rationalizes their dishonesty.

Crosses?
Signifies twisted rationalizing of one's actions and motives.

Horizontals?

Stress indicating lack of common sense and barriers to the free application of logic and reason.

The Thumb, Phalange Three
(The Mount of Venus)

Does the phalange have . . .

Verticals?

Vitality; intense emotional and physical feelings; a love of life, relationships, and family. This also can signify assistance given to the subject by others in a close, supportive relationship.

Grilles?

A mark of one with a passionate disposition, yet with some confusion regarding sexual and emotional priorities.

Crosses?

A sign of emotional obsession. (The traditional reading is of "an only love; a single, all-absorbing passion.")

Horizontals?

A sign of stress, usually indicating interference or influence of another in sexual and family relationships.

The Major Lines

Life Line

The life line, also called the vital, represents the physical self and shows general health, vitality, and physical interaction with the environment (see Figure 24).

Is the line . . .

Clear, well-defined, and long-reaching, or almost reaching the wrist?

This signifies health, vitality, and energy. It also shows the optimism and positive outlook of someone with good coping skills who adapts well to changes. It promises a long and generally healthy life.

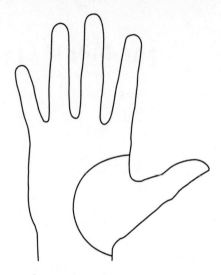

Figure 24: The life line

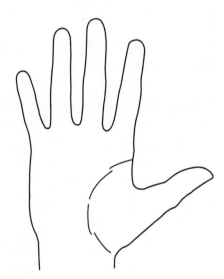

Figure 25: A broken life line

Broken in one or more places?
Breaks signify disruptions to the physical self. They can also be an indication of acute illness or a sudden change in circumstances, such as the quitting of an old lifestyle and the beginning of a new one. The change may be positive or negative, depending on the condition of the line after the break (see Figure 25).

Very broken, with chains, ladders, or fraying?
This is a sign of uncertain health, low vitality and energy levels, exhaustion, and poor powers of recuperation. It suggests a life of much disruption, change, and difficulty (see Figure 26).

Marked with islands?
Islands are traditionally negative and indicate periods of ill health. They may also represent periods of split energy, which can occur when the subject is experiencing a period of discontentment due to an unhappy marriage, unpleasant work, and so on (see Figure 27).

Apparently double, with parallel lines?
This is a sign of strength, an enduring constitution, and strong recuperative powers. It may also indicate dissatisfaction with routine, a need to continually seek changes in circumstances, restlessness, and a need of personal freedom. It can signify the extent of spiritual and emotional support given by a companion or spouse who provides love and assistance, and the degree to which the subject is dependent on that person.

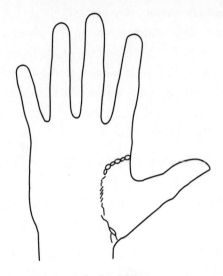

Figure 26: A very broken life line

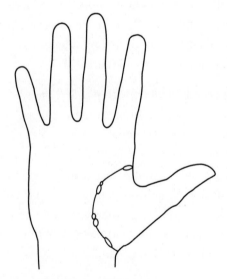

Figure 27: Life line with islands

It also tells of an intense sexual and emotional life. When the life line is clearly double, the subject has an inner and an outer life that are distinctly separate. This is occasionally found in people with jobs that require a professional persona (see Figure 28).

Crossed by small lines?
These are lines of influence, and usually represent other people. This influence may be negative or positive.

If there are many lines, they indicate the susceptibility of the subject to influence, betraying a submissive personality or a lack of self-confidence (see Figure 29).

Short—only reaching the center of the palm?
A short life line, contrary to popular myth, does not mean a short life. The length of the life line is related more to a person's energy levels than to time or the length of life.

When short and thick, it indicates intense energy but a relatively incident-free life. This may mean a monotonous life, but it can also show that the subject has ceased to accept the challenges of life, and has become somewhat withdrawn or self-absorbed.

If the line is short and thin, faded or broken, poor health and withdrawal of social life may be the subject's challenge (see Figure 30).

Long—reaching the wrist?
This is a sign of great physical vitality, with good powers of recuperation; there is the probability of a long and healthy life with an optimistic, healthy outlook (see Figure 31).

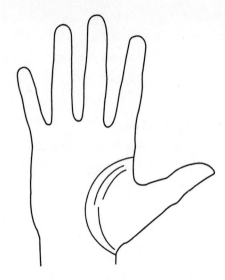

Figure 28: *An apparently double life line*

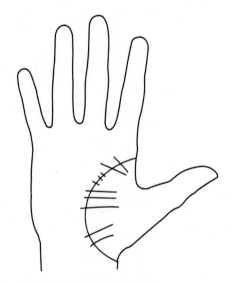

Figure 29: *A life line crossed by small lines*

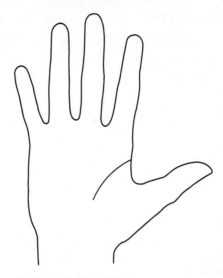

Figure 30: A short life line

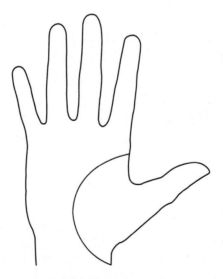

Figure 31: A long life line

Thick and red?

This shows a high level of physical vitality and energy. If very red, a physical, possibly violent, nature, irritable and excitable (see Figure 32).

Pale and thin?

This marks low levels of physical vitality and energy, weakness due to stress generated by personal problems, and poor health due to lack of vitamins or essential body salts (see Figure 33).

Slightly curved, clinging to the base of the thumb?

This is a sign of one who is family oriented and fond of domestic life. It may also indicate restriction, discontentment, and a lack of warmth and vitality. This person may be timid, conservative, and uninterested in change and travel (see Figure 34).

Steeply curved, reaching well into the palm?

A desire to travel, dislike of routine and restrictions, and a sustained, conscious effort toward personal freedom are all indicated by this type of line.

It also shows a life strongly influenced by emotion and the subconscious, and indicates vitality, resilience, and warmth of one who may be inclined toward a spiritual search for truth (see Figure 35).

Does the line . . .

Change direction suddenly?

This represents distinct changes in the direction, aims, or purpose of the life (see Figure 36).

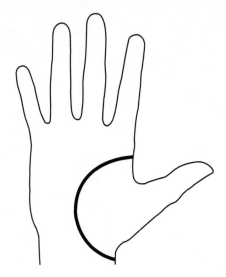

Figure 32: A thick life line

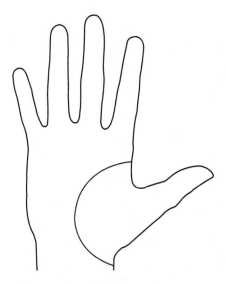

Figure 33: A thin life line

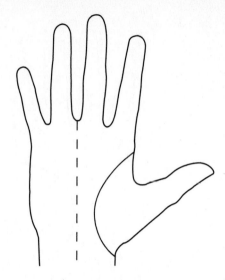

Figure 34: A slightly curved life line

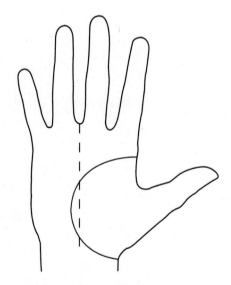

Figure 35: A steeply curved life line

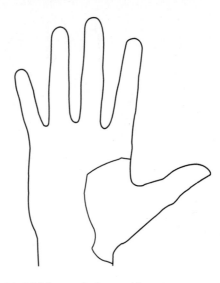

Figure 36: A life line with changing directions

Begin touching the head line?
Touching for less than one centimeter: This is a mark of average mental and physical development, with a strong family influence in childhood.

Touching for more than one centimeter: This is a sign of lack of independence, restrictions in early life due to parental domination, self-consciousness, and lack of self-confidence.

This can also indicate health, educational, or environmental problems—a subject cautious and reserved, with a fear of commitment. The longer the join, the greater the above characteristics and influence (see Figure 37).

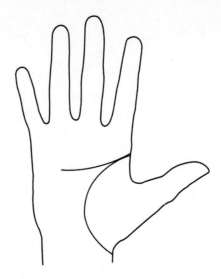

Figure 37: *The life line beginning
joined with the head line*

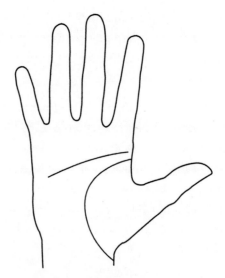

Figure 38: *The life line beginning
apart from the head line*

Begin well separated from the head line?
This signals independence and a need for personal freedom. An impulsive person holding firm opinions, this individual is energetic and self-reliant, with managerial talents.

If very widely separated, there may be a lack of self-discipline, and the ideals of independence may be taken to extremes, resulting in rash action, foolhardiness, and impatience—grand ideas but very little action.

A fine network of lines between the life and the head lines usually indicates family resistance to the individuality and independence of the subject (see Figure 38).

Begin above the head line?
This is a sign of a cautious, timid nature, prone to worry and lacking self-confidence; someone who is too open to influence and domination by others and whose intellectual energy is underemployed. Often irritable, the subject is generally ruled by emotion rather than logic and reason (see Figure 39).

Begin with an irregularity, branch, or island?
A sign of childhood weakness. This may be an indication of health, or a record of adverse environmental influences (see Figure 40).

End well across the palm, toward the percussion (i.e., the edge of the hand)?
Wanderlust, restlessness, and travel are all indicated. The subject may be disinclined toward family life, disliking routine and seeking change. This can also indicate spiritual leanings (see Figure 41).

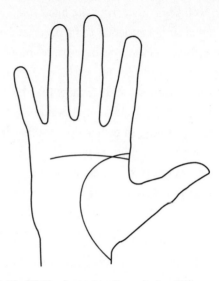

Figure 39: The life line beginning above the head line

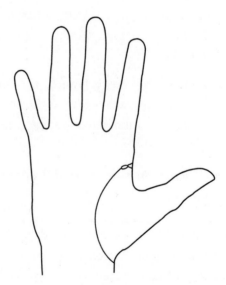

Figure 40: The life line beginning with an irregularity

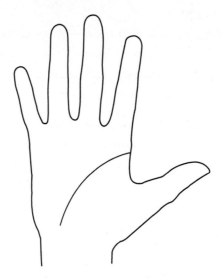

Figure 41: The life line ending near the percussion

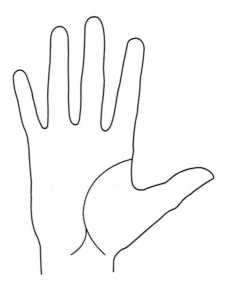

Figure 42: The life line ending in a fork

End in a fork?

Signifies possible changes in old age, general restlessness, and a love for—indeed, need of—travel and change. It may also indicate a late bloomer, meaning increased possibilities in late middle age (see Figure 42).

Branch upward, toward the fingers?

A symbol of replenished energy and happiness due to increases in influence and personal power. This may also indicate an effort to further personal ambitions or to improve oneself (see Figure 43).

Branch down, toward the wrist?

This shows a diminishing or splitting of vital physical energy. It may signal a difficulty or a loss—personal or material (see Figure 44).

Head Line

This line, also called the mental, represents the intellectual self and shows the degree and character of the intelligence, reasoning powers, and ability to concentrate and learn, as well as mental activity in general.

Is the line . . .

Clear, well-defined, and long? (The line is long if it reaches more than halfway across the palm.)

A sign of mental energy, intelligence, a good physical and mental constitution, a clear thinker, and one who can reach rational conclusions (see Figure 45).

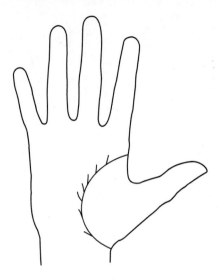

Figure 43: Life line branching upward, toward the fingers

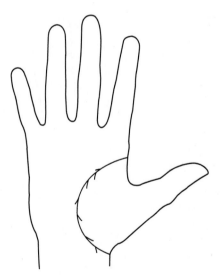

Figure 44: Life line branching downward, toward the wrist

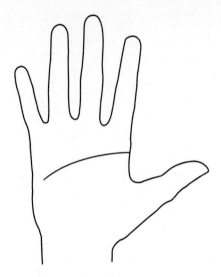

Figure 45: A well-defined head line

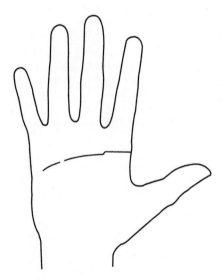

Figure 46: A broken head line

Broken in one or more places?

Breaks tend to impede thinking, affect the ability to concentrate, and can indicate mental stress or breakdown. They can also represent a complete change in the way of thinking: a shift from an established viewpoint to a new set of mental values. Furthermore, breaks can indicate a physical injury to the head, or a severe shock (see Figure 46).

Very broken, with chains, ladders, or fraying?

A sign of an inability to concentrate or reach rational conclusions. An indecisive and easily distracted subject who lacks continuity of ideas, and so appears to be changeable and fickle. The subject may be prone to mood swings.

This can also be an indication of acute trauma or severe mental stress (see Figure 47).

Marked with islands?

Islands represent a split in energy flow, and thus represent a period of difficulty and confusion, with much indecision and uncertainty. They can also represent trauma, whether it be actual psychosis, mental breakdown, or head injury (see Figure 48).

Very straight?

Signifies numeracy, a materialistic outlook, and rational judgment; a person who is generally analytical in their outlook and approach to life, and who is incisive and decisive, with application to detail.

This subject may have a tendency to ignore or discount emotional considerations when making decisions (see Figure 49).

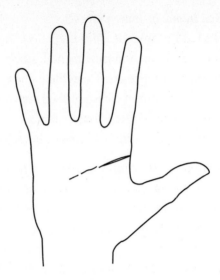

Figure 47: A very broken head line

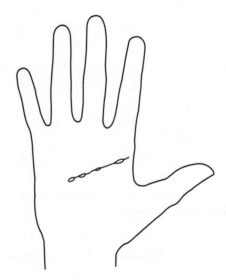

Figure 48: A head line marked with islands

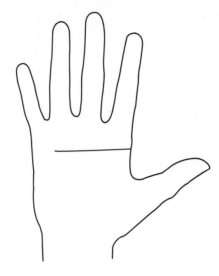

Figure 49: A very straight head line

Curved, either up or down?
Curved up: This shows a practical, materialistic mentality—a mind for business.

Curved down: A mark of imagination. The steeper the curve, the greater the influence of the subconscious mind upon the life. A gentle curve indicates a vivid and versatile imagination, with a tendency to daydream. When the curve is very steep, the subconscious influence is powerful. It can show a tendency to withdraw from everyday reality and can indicate (a) potential or actual mental problems due to an overactive imagination, (b) artistic and creative ability, or (c) deep spirituality (see Figure 50).

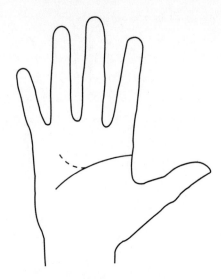

Figure 50: *A head line may curve upward (dashed line)
or downward (solid line)*

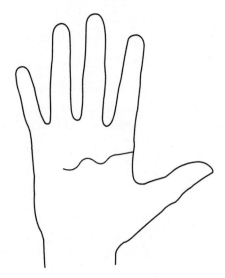

Figure 51: *An erratic head line*

Changing direction suddenly?

This suggests an erratic, changeable mentality. The subject may use odd reasoning methods in decision making, confusing the obvious and pertinent with the obscure and irrelevant. Possibly superstitious, the subject may place great emphasis on unimportant factors, making behavior difficult to understand (see Figure 51).

Very long—reaching more than halfway across the palm?

The line is long if it ends beneath fingers three or four. This shows the subject to be intelligent, observant, understanding, and in possession of a positive outlook on life, with a keen sense of logic and good learning abilities (see Figure 52).

Very short—not reaching more than halfway across the palm?

Someone with fixed ideas who takes a strictly practical approach to matters rather than a visionary, imaginative attitude. Sometimes it indicates a thinker who lacks curiosity, and doesn't look past the surface appearances (see Figure 53).

Joined to the heart line, so that it makes one line reaching across the entire palm?

Here the streams of intellectual and emotional energy have joined, giving great mental energy, emotional intensity, and stamina. The result is an intense, headstrong, and self-willed personality who feels a need for total commitment in work, play, and relationships.

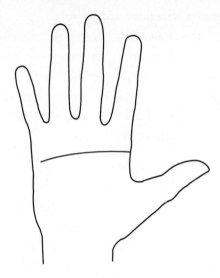

Figure 52: A long head line

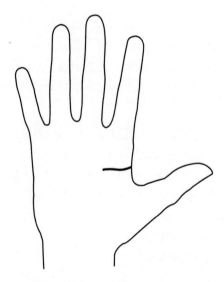

Figure 53: A short head line

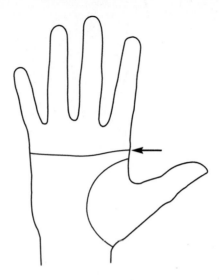

Figure 54: A joined head and heart line

There may at times be a confusion of energies, and of logic and emotions. The subject may tend to "think" with feelings and "feel" through logic, leading to inappropriate behavior, e.g., an emotional manager, a rational lover (see Figure 54).

So long that it crosses the entire palm?

This is symptomatic of a self divided into emotional and intellectual halves, leading to strictly logical reasoning with no emotional input, or emotional behavior with no logical input.

Great insight is indicated, and an ability to reason without emotional interruption; however, problems may arise from this lack of integration between emotional and logical

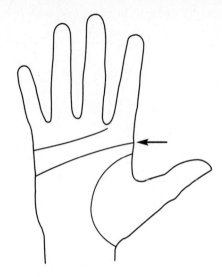

Figure 55: A head line crossing entire palm

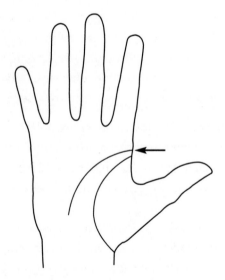

Figure 56: The head line parallel to the life line

considerations, and this often results in the suppression of the emotional and imaginative aspects of the personality.

Traditionally, this is an indication of high intelligence that can lead to fame (see Figure 55).

Steeply curved, so that it runs parallel to the life line?
The influence of the subconscious is very powerful in the subject with this feature, and this can lead to oversensitivity or paranoia, along with some confusion between the imagined and reality. It often indicates (a) artistic and creative powers; (b) potential or actual mental problems; or (c) deep spirituality, with possible psychic or clairvoyant powers (see Figure 56).

Red?
This is a sign of a dynamic and strong will. If very red, high energy verging on hyperactivity is indicated and, possibly, a violent nature.

Very pale?
This indicates mental fatigue and lack of energy, and possibly a lack of essential body salts. The subject may be under psychological stress.

Does the line . . .
Begin touching the life line?
Shows normal mental development in childhood; a good start to life (see Figure 57).

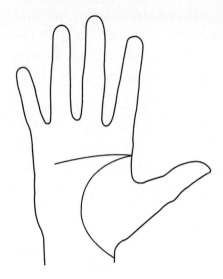

Figure 57: Head line beginning at life line

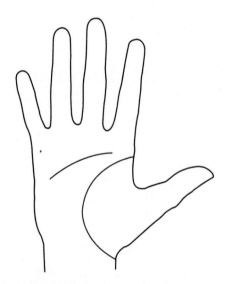

*Figure 58: Head line beginning well into the palm
and separated from the life line*

Begin separated from the life line and well into the palm?

A lack of positive formative influences is suggested, along with a lack of family pride or involvement.

Possibly a late developer, the subject may be uninterested in conventional achievement (see Figure 58).

End in a fork?

Denotes great imagination via conscious access to subconscious processes, and an ability to make dreams come true. This is also a sign of artistic ability and creativity, and is traditionally called the poet's or writer's fork.

The subject is capable of viewing situations from two sides, which can mean duplicity.

If the fork is very steep and long, it may indicate an overactive imagination with its attendant problems, or a leaning toward spirituality, with some psychic ability (see Figure 59).

End curved up at the tip?

Signals a desire for material gain from someone with a practical turn of mind and business acumen (see Figure 60).

Heart Line

This line, also called the mensal, represents the emotional self and shows the degree and type of emotional experience, and the way it is expressed. It is located directly beneath the fingers, beginning on the percussion and ending somewhere in the region beneath the first and second fingers.

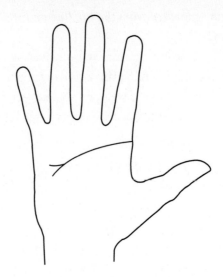

Figure 59: The poet's or writer's fork

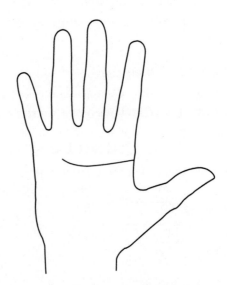

Figure 60: A head line ending curved up at the tip

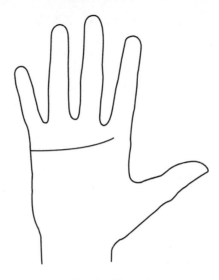

Figure 61: A well-defined heart line

Is the line . . .

Clear, well-defined, and long? (The heart line is long if it reaches more than halfway across the palm.)

The subject is capable of strong, firm affections and self-sacrifice in relationships. He or she will be emotionally mature and self-confident.

There is a probability of a lifestyle that promotes stable relationships and has spiritual purpose (see Figure 61).

Broken in one or more places?

A sign of a break in the flow of emotional energy; a change in emotional attachments, which may indicate disappointment or disillusionment in love; can indicate, quite literally, a broken heart (see Figure 62).

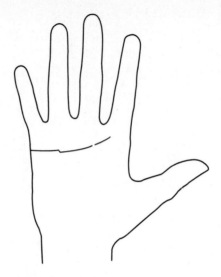

Figure 62: A broken heart line

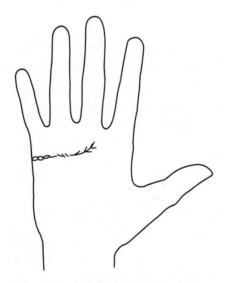

Figure 63: A very broken heart line,
with chains, ladders, and fraying

Very broken, with chains, ladders, or fraying?

The subject is emotionally immature or uncertain, lacks love for self, and is unconvinced of his or her own attractiveness.

This subject is attracted to novelty and change, needs constantly to renew excitement, and is likely to be fickle (see Figure 63).

Marked with islands?

These are a sign of insecurity or of someone who is always actively seeking fulfillment. Brooding periods with depression are symptomatic of this characteristic, along with an active discontent with relationships.

A single island is a sign of divided energies. One can consider the palm as a sort of circuit board, with the lines as lines of current. An island represents split or divided energies and, on the heart line, it might be a period of divided loyalties.

Many islands can indicate a flirtatious character—a person who perhaps has many affairs. It can sometimes indicate a contempt for the opposite sex (arising out of contempt for self), and difficulty in trusting a sexual partner, again due to mistrust of self.

This may also indicate a heart condition (see Figure 64).

Intersected by short, small lines?

The number of these small influence lines is a measure of the influence of others upon the subject—or of the subject's capacity to be influenced.

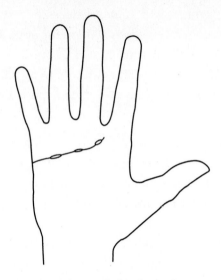

Figure 64: A heart line marked with islands

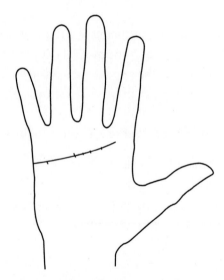

Figure 65: A heart line with influence lines

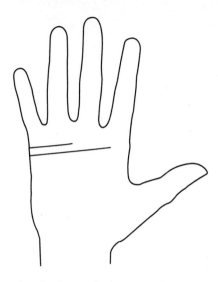

Figure 66: Examples of a short and a long, straight heart line

They can also represent a constantly shifting emotional focus (hence the traditional reading of promiscuity), inconstancy, and a series of flirtatious affairs (see Figure 65).

Quite straight?
If short: A sign of calculating, undemonstrative emotional nature; selfish sensuality.

If long (reaching to base of finger one): Signifies a humanistic, idealistic, and undemonstrative emotional nature; someone whose response tends to be intellectual rather than emotional, yet is usually erotic (see Figure 66).

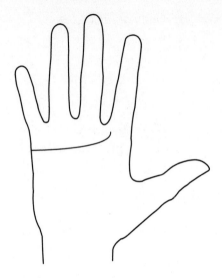

Figure 67: A heart line curved at the end

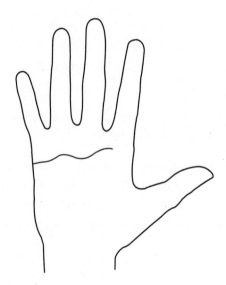

Figure 68: A heart line with direction changes

Curved (especially at the end)?

Signals a warm, impulsive, and physically demonstrative nature; one with a strong need to express affection physically and sexually, and who may be jealous and possessive (see Figure 67).

Changing direction suddenly?

This can indicate a change in the basic emotional nature, along with obscure emotional reasoning whereby trivialities become confused with more important considerations.

This can make the subject's emotional decisions and reactions difficult for others to understand (see Figure 68).

Very pale?

A sign of low energy levels, unless it is the subject's natural complexion. It may also indicate a lack of essential vitamins, minerals, or body salts.

Red in color?

This suggests high levels of emotional energy—an emotionally passionate, intense, and possibly violent nature. There may also be an indication of a cardiac condition or high blood pressure.

Does the line . . .

Begin at the percussion (i.e., the edge of the hand)?

This is a sign of the normal emotional development of a sentimental person, one who is capable of giving and taking and loving (see Figure 69).

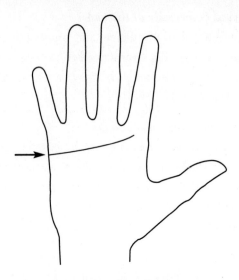

Figure 69: Heart line beginning at the percussion

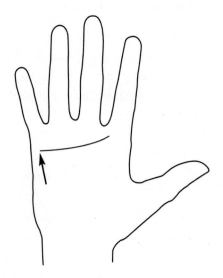

Figure 70: Heart line beginning into the palm

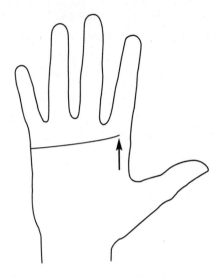

Figure 71: Heart line ending under finger one

Begin anywhere other than the percussion?

Indicates some interference with early emotional development, like a disturbance of emotional character that has had a lasting influence. It can mean the subject has developed a calculating, emotionally self-centered nature as a form of self-preservation (see Figure 70).

End under finger one?

This typifies the reliable, devoted type with a capacity for one consuming love. Faithful and devoted to the highest ideals of humanistic love, this person may nevertheless be undemonstrative. Easily hurt due to idealism on the battlefield of love, he or she is generally an affectionate, happy, and free person (see Figure 71).

End between fingers one and two?

This represents the ideal: one with a warm, generous, sympathetic, and affectionate nature. Tending toward physical displays of emotions and an active role in relationships, this is a healthy balance between romantic idealism and sensuality.

This person has an affinity for long-term relationships, such as marriage. They may also be somewhat possessive and even jealous. This is quite normal and healthy, if kept within reason (see Figure 72).

End under finger two?

An unsentimental and undemonstrative person, for whom emotion figures in a minor key.

This personality is likely to have no strong feelings for others, and possess an element of unsentimental, self-centered sensuality in sexual relationships (see Figure 73).

End under finger three?

This person may feel little emotion and be extremely cautious when it comes to emotional involvement, possibly due to lack of strong emotional drive.

He or she may feel the need to maintain distance within a relationship and may be entirely motivated by sexual reasons (see Figure 74).

End in a fork?

This is a sign that love and involvement are important to the subject, who is emotionally intense.

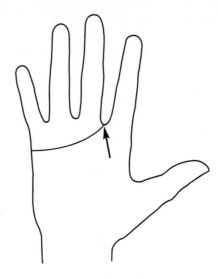

*Figure 72: Heart line ending between
fingers one and two*

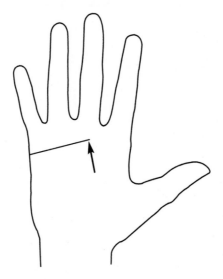

Figure 73: Heart line ending under finger two

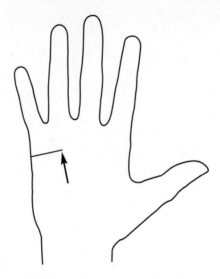

Figure 74: Heart line ending under finger three

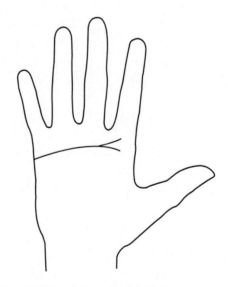

Figure 75: Heart line ending in a fork

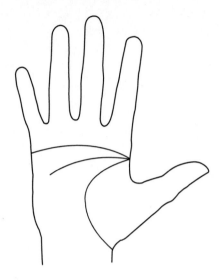

Figure 76: Heart line joined to head line

The person with this feature is likely to possess strong, honest feelings, and very often has a humanitarian outlook.

A triple fork (trident) is considered a very fortunate sign that the subject is capable of happy and passionate romantic attachments (see Figure 75).

End joined to the head line?

A sign of confused reason, emotion, and instinct. This is often the mark of an emotionally dependent person in need of constant support, approval, and affection from a partner.

He or she is most likely to be very sensitive to atmosphere and nuance (see Figure 76).

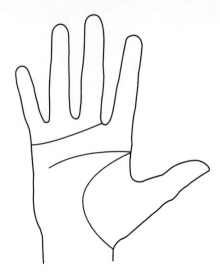

Figure 77: Heart line closer to fingers than to head line

Lie closer to the fingers than to the head line?

Shows a wide gap between emotional and intellectual energies. This can lead to a lifestyle dictated by logic and reason, with little emotional input, or, conversely, to one based on emotions, with little intellectual input (see Figure 77).

Fate Line

This line, also called the Saturnian, represents career and material achievement. It is also known as the career line, or the path-of-life line. This line can be difficult to locate, as it often exists in fragmentary form and is easily confused with other lines. The best way to locate it is to trace it downward from the base of finger two. Many people do not have a fate line.

Is the line . . .

Absent?

This is a sign that the subject has no discernible path in life and is not forced or constrained to follow any particular path by family, or influences of education and environment. He or she is likely to have the attitude of taking life as it comes.

In a weak hand, it indicates an aimless outlook—a character overly subject to outside influence.

Clear, long, and well-defined?

Indicates a single, direct, and straight path through life.

The subject probably has a strong sense of duty, coupled with a fatalistic, determined attitude. This is also called the career line, as it can indicate the probability of success in a material sense and in the sphere of business. However, it can also simply mean the following of a single life path, whether it leads to success or not (see Figure 78).

Broken in one or more places?

Breaks represent changes in the career or life path. Many breaks show many changes, which can be negative or positive. How the line continues after each break indicates how the change has been adapted to (see Figure 79).

Marked with islands?

Islands are usually negative. They indicate split energies, and here signal a temporary weakening effect.

They are also a sign of stress, showing difficulties in the career (see Figure 80).

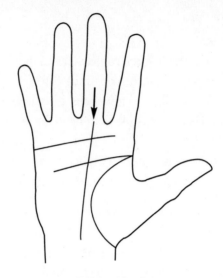

Figure 78: A well-defined fate line

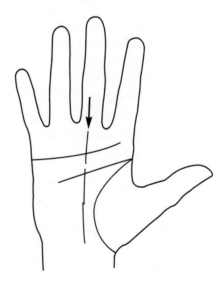

Figure 79: A fate line broken in more than one place

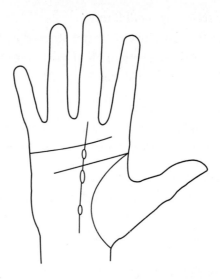

Figure 80: A fate line marked with islands

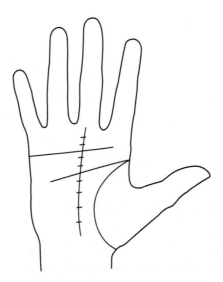

Figure 81: A fate line intersected by small lines

Intersected by small lines?
A sign of a sensitive character stressed by the demands of career or chosen path of life. This person may appear to be distant and detached (see Figure 81).

Very curved or bent?
This signifies, literally, a curved and bent path through life, with many changes of direction (see Figure 82).

Double, or with parallel lines?
A mark of versatility or of skills that may lead to a double career, and of more than one path or career being pursued at one time (see Figure 83).

Does the line . . .

Begin right at the base of the palm, so that it runs the length of the palm?
This is an indication of a strong genetic or cultural inheritance. The subject has been following his or her predetermined path since birth (see Figure 84).

Begin in the middle of the palm?
This represents the start of a career, or of some particular course (such as a spiritual direction), or the discovery and embracing of a lifestyle, which occurs in the early to mid-twenties (see Figure 85).

Begin in contact with the life line?
This shows an inheritance—genetic or family—that creates a life path, and expectation or pressure by family and relatives to follow a predetermined career.

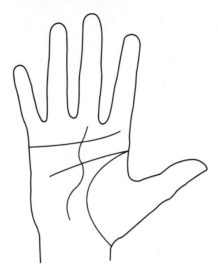

Figure 82: A curved fate line

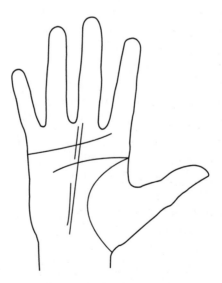

Figure 83: A fate line with double or parallel lines

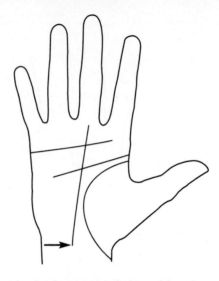

Figure 84: A fate line beginning at the base of the palm

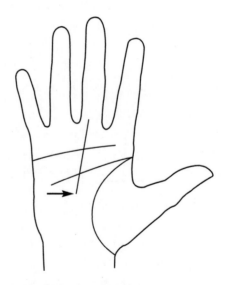

Figure 85: A fate line beginning
in the middle of the palm

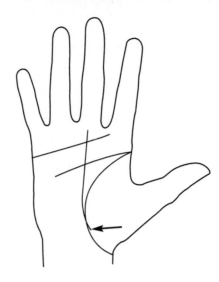

*Figure 86: A fate line beginning in contact
with the life line*

It can also indicate domination by parents, family, or spouse (see Figure 86).

Begin with a fork?
A small fork at the very beginning shows that a choice was available at the beginning. A larger fork, with the joining point higher in the palm, shows the entrance into the life of a major influence.

It is often an indication of marriage (see Figure 87).

Begin on mount eight (mount of the moon)?
Denotes one who needs to express creativity, and who is hopeful and imaginative. The career of this person will depend on others to succeed (e.g., public life, show business,

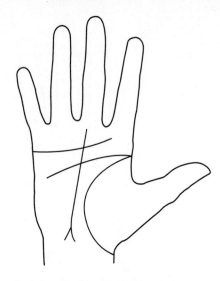

Figure 87: A fate line beginning with a fork

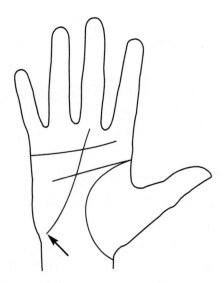

Figure 88: A fate line beginning on mount eight

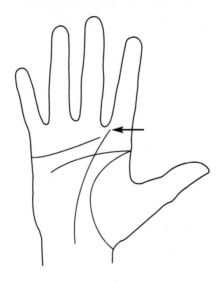

Figure 89: A fate line ending under finger one

sports). May be unconventional and adventurous, with a love of travel and change.

The subject may also be largely unaware of his or her true motivation and ambitions, and can at times be deeply spiritual (see Figure 88).

End under finger one?
Shows driving ambition that is gratified at the end of a determined path, and a strong probability of material and career success (see Figure 89).

End under finger two?
Indicates a probability of career success; an ability to take advantage of opportunities. This is the usual termination point of the line (see Figure 90).

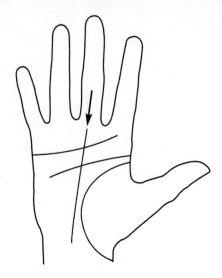

Figure 90: Fate line ending under finger two

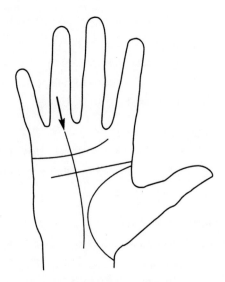

Figure 91: Fate line ending under finger three

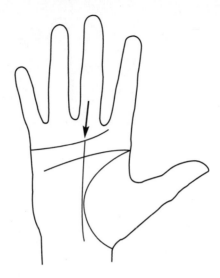

Figure 92: Fate line ending at the heart line

End under finger three?

Artistic ambitions and career are indicated, probably talent in the area of literature, art, or music; inclination toward an artistic lifestyle (see Figure 91).

End under the heart line?

This signals a career or life path interrupted or curtailed by emotional considerations, such as stress engendered by career success (see Figure 92).

End at the head line?

Depending on other aspects of the hand, this can signify (a) a career or life path interrupted or curtailed by intellectual considerations or stress engendered by success in career, or (b) someone whose life is strictly controlled by parents or spouse (see Figure 93).

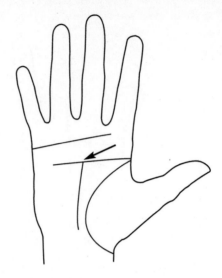

Figure 93: Fate line ending at the head line

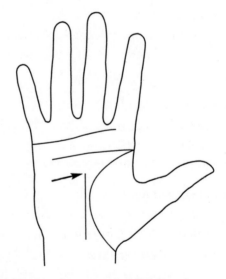

Figure 94: Fate line ending in the middle of the palm

End in the middle of the palm?

This may mean the subject has succeeded in breaking out of a narrow, restricting life path, and achieved freedom of choice.

However, the traditional reading is of career failure after a good start; a failure to recognize or exploit opportunities (see Figure 94).

Sun Line

This line, also called the Apollo line, traditionally represents artistic success and recognition. It is also called the line of brilliance and is related to probability of achievement and the attainment of contentment. Like the fate line, it can be quite difficult to locate. Although it runs up the palm, the best way to locate it is to trace it downward from the base of finger three. It generally exists in a fragmentary form. Many people do not have a sun line.

Is the line . . .

Absent?

Subjects without a sun line may have creative talent and artistic ability, but need to develop qualities such as business acumen and ambition if they wish to achieve recognition and success in the creative arts.

Clear, long, and well-defined?

The subject is capable of success and recognition in a chosen field, particularly the creative arts, and is a basically happy, contented person.

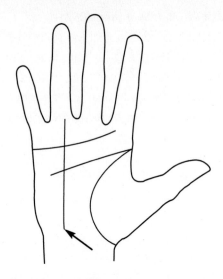

Figure 95: A well-defined sun line

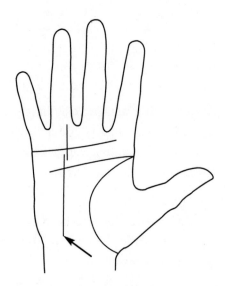

Figure 96: A broken sun line

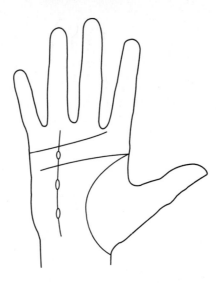

Figure 97: Sun line marked with islands

A sign, also, of successful application of natural talent and brilliance—hence the traditional name, the line of brilliance (see Figure 95).

Broken in one or more places?
Denotes interruptions or breaks in the progress of artistic development and evolution, a scattering or dissipation of artistic energy, and hindrances to recognition and success (see Figure 96).

Marked with islands?
A sign of split energies, distraction and dissatisfaction, and of problems that interfere with career and artistic development.

The traditional reading is of loss of position, and scandal (see Figure 97).

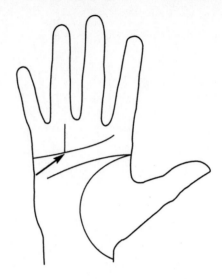

Figure 98: Sun line beginning at the heart line

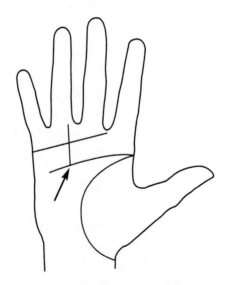

Figure 99: Sun line beginning at the head line

Begin at the heart line?

Signifies the capable application of knowledge (often eso-teric) gained in early life, leading to a measure of fame and success in middle age. This is the mark of a lateral thinker who makes major decisions based on emotional considera-tions. A late starter whose influence has taken time to grow, the subject probably isn't particularly ambitious in the conventional sense, has a love of art and beauty, and probably little interest in material gain (see Figure 98).

Begin at the head line?

A sign of probable success and recognition, beginning in early middle age (around forty years). Some traditions call this a sign of genius, suggesting that success arises from some intellectual inspiration or effort (see Figure 99).

Begin at the life line?

This represents probable success that is fostered with assis-tance from parents or family, or by some inheritance, ge-netic or otherwise (see Figure 100).

Begin at the fate line?

This signals a new life path that arises from the career or the normal life path of the subject. It could be a hobby that gradually takes over, or some other passionate interest that takes more and more time and energy. This can also repre-sent an emergence, after repression, of artistic talents and ambitions (see Figure 101).

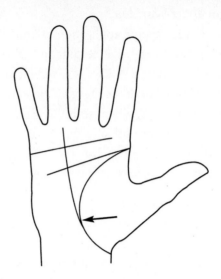

Figure 100: Sun line beginning at the life line

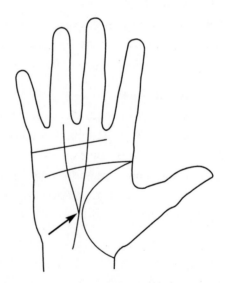

Figure 101: Sun line beginning at the fate line

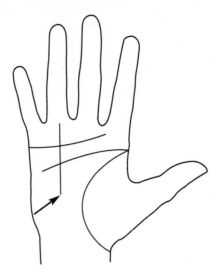

Figure 102: Sun line beginning in the center of the palm

Begin in the center of the palm?

A sign that the life path or artistic career of the subject does not start until his or her mid-twenties. Difficulties in choosing a path that satisfies creative leanings are also indicated (see Figure 102).

End at the base of finger three?

The subject possesses qualities and talents that make artistic recognition and creative success a strong probability (see Figure 103).

End at the heart line?

This represents a creative path abandoned due to emotional stress that may be the result of either success or failure and frustration in working life (see Figure 104).

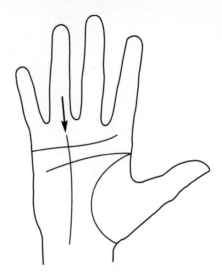

Figure 103: Sun line ending at the base of finger three

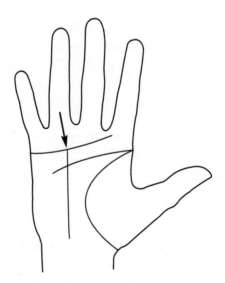

Figure 104: Sun line ending at heart line

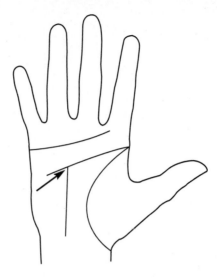

Figure 105: Sun line ending at the head line

It can also indicate a tendency to base crucial decisions on emotional considerations, often to the detriment of the practical.

End at the head line?
Represents a creative path abandoned due to mental and intellectual stress resulting from success or failure and frustration in working life (see Figure 105).

End in a fork?
A sign of additional subjects or interests taken up in middle age and maturity. Traditional readings suggest outstanding success and recognition, and probable wealth (see Figure 106).

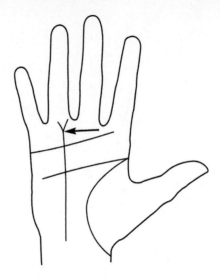

Figure 106: Sun line ending in a fork

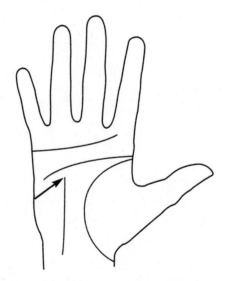

Figure 107: Sun line ending in the middle of the palm

End in the middle of the palm, below the head line?

A creative pathway fades out. Tradition has it that this is a sign of early success, followed by stagnation (see Figure 107).

Union Line

There may be one or more of these union lines, also called the marriage lines, arising on the side of the hand (the percussion) between the base of the little finger and the heart line. These lines usually represent a deep emotional attachment to a person, but may also signal the ability or maturity to commit, as well as an actual commitment to a career or a cause.

Is the line . . .

Absent?

A mark of emotional immaturity. The subject is currently incapable of making a major emotional commitment to a person or cause.

Straight and clear?

This is the ideal line, representing happy, intense, and generally satisfying emotional involvement and commitment. Traditionally this means a happy marriage.

More than one line does not necessarily imply more than one marriage, as the union line can also represent commitment to a career or a cause (see Figure 108).

Cut by fine lines?

A sign of obstacles and opposition in emotional relationships. These lines can also represent fertility or the desire to have children. Tradition has it that lines that go up toward the fingers indicate boys, and lines that go down show girls (see Figure 109).

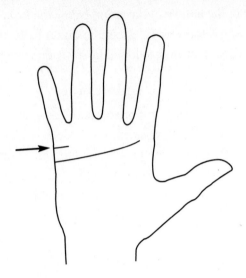

Figure 108: A clear union line

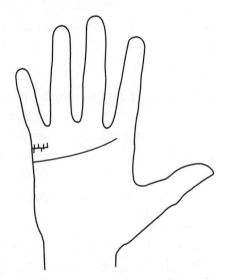

Figure 109: Union line intersected by fine lines

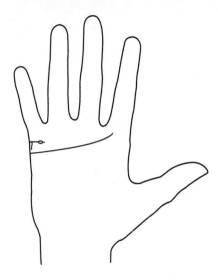

Figure 110: Union line marked with islands

Marked by islands?

Islands indicate problems and difficulties in the relationship; possibly enforced separation, or split loyalties (see Figure 110).

Does the line . . .

End in a fork?

This signifies an extreme, intense form of emotional commitment, possibly a marriage with many quarrels or disagreements, or a love/hate relationship.

It can also imply a broken commitment, or an unhappy relationship that ends in separation.

This is also a sign of waning sexual interest in marriage, or disillusionment with a commitment (see Figure 111).

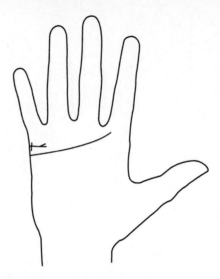

Figure 111: Union line ending in a fork

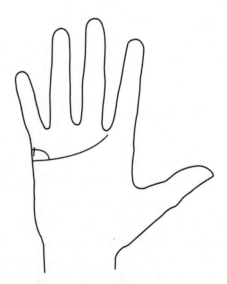

*Figure 112: Union line ending in a
downward curve, toward the heart line*

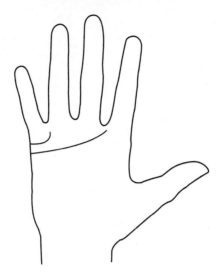

Figure 113: Union line ending with an upward curve

End with a downward curve, toward the heart line?

Represents enforced separation; a person who has difficulties maintaining their commitment. Traditionally this has signified widowhood (see Figure 112).

End with an upward curve, toward the fingers?

The subject is unlikely to stick with major emotional commitments. The difficulty in maintaining relationships arises out of conditioning, education, or experience (see Figure 113).

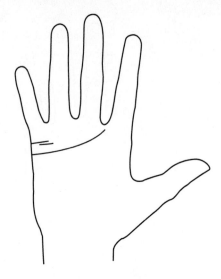

Figure 114: Union line with a parallel line

Have a fine line, parallel and close by?

A sign of an emotional commitment made shortly after marriage. It may indicate a person, a cause, or a career. It often indicates commitment to children (see Figure 114).

Hepatic Line

This line, also called the health line, the liver line, and the hepatica, can represent a health condition or a preoccupation with health. This line may be difficult to locate and is best traced downward from beneath the fourth finger. Unlike the sun and fate lines, it runs diagonally across the palm.

Some traditions call this the line of Mercury, and regard it as the business line, to be read as an indication of a person's business life, following the normal rules that apply to reading lines.

Is the line . . .

Absent?

The absence of the hepatica, or health line, is considered a positive indication regarding health and constitution. Furthermore, business is not a major concern in the subject's life.

Long, straight, and well-defined?

Here is a warning of some chronic health problem. (The traditional meaning is of liver and digestive problems.) It can also signal one who is overly conscious of their health, and is possibly a hypochondriac.

In addition, it may be a sign of healing ability, most notably when the line forms a clear triangle in the center of the palm with the head and fate or life lines.

This person has a probable talent for business, and a strong possibility for success in business (see Figure 115).

Very curved and/or bent?

Suggests liver problems and digestive difficulties that may promote irritability and bad temper; generally poor health.

Trade and business do not run smoothly for this person (see Figure 116).

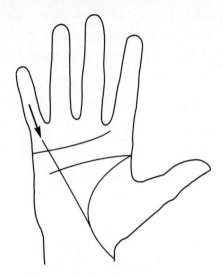

Figure 115: A well-defined hepatic line

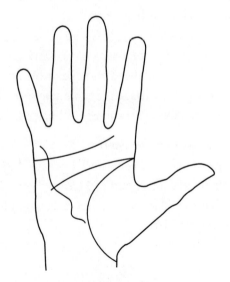

Figure 116: A curved hepatic line

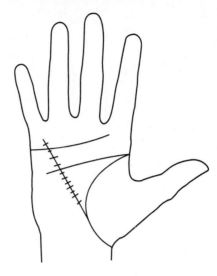

Figure 117: A hepatic line crossed by fine lines

Pale and wide?
Chronic digestion problems; poor circulation. A slow-moving career is indicated, as is hard work with minimal profits.

Red?
Cardiac problems. A difficult business life.

Crossed by small lines?
Migraine headaches. A business life beset by many problems and difficulties (see Figure 117).

Does the line . . .

Have islands?
Chronic respiratory problems. Major setbacks in business; prolonged periods of recession (see Figure 118).

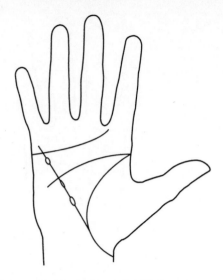

Figure 118: Hepatic line with islands

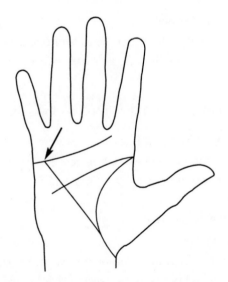

Figure 119: Hepatic line beginning at the heart line

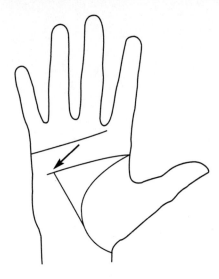

Figure 120: Hepatic line beginning at the head line

Begin at the heart line?

Cardiac problems. Indicates a hobby or interest that has become a business (see Figure 119).

Begin at the head line?

A sign of nervous tension and susceptibility to stress (see Figure 120).

The Mounts

The mounts are raised areas on the palm that represent different areas of the psyche, e.g., the libido, the subconscious, and so forth. Development (or the lack of) in the mounts sounds a base note by which all the other characteristics of the hand are modified. Sometimes, one or two mounts will be larger or more prominent than the rest, and clearly indicate the major motivating energy in the subject.

Take the subject's hand and examine each mount by touch as well as sight (see Figure 121 for mount location).

Mount One:
Jupiter/Saturn
(see Figure 122)

Is the mount . . .

Well-developed, firm, and high?
A sign of positive masculine qualities, corresponding to the yang principle and to the animus, this signifies personal power, pride, ambition, and competitiveness.

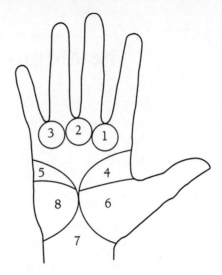

Figure 121: The mounts

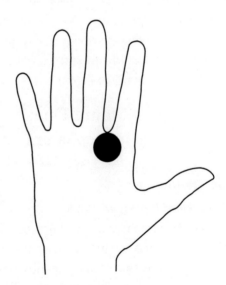

Figure 122: Mount one

This person has strong willpower, executive skills, and personal ambition that can lead to a high position. In addition, he or she has a love of art, ritual, and information.

Overdeveloped?

A sign of there being too much yang in the personality: the masculine qualities dominate, often to the detriment of the yin aspects, resulting in a lack of balance. This challenges the subject to be less selfish and to be more considerate of others, and be aware that the purely hormonal qualities of masculinity need to be tempered by softer qualities.

Other side effects can include cynicism and morbidity.

Undeveloped, flat, or hollow?

This signifies undeveloped masculine qualities. He or she may be uncompetitive in the conventional sense, and nonauthoritarian.

Crossed by vertical lines?

A sign of one attempting to improve his or her material position, in whom positive energy manifests as ambition or a striving toward some goal (see Figure 123).

If the fate line ends in this area, a strong probability of success is indicated.

Crossed by horizontal lines?

These are stress lines and show difficulties in the spheres of ambition or work (see Figure 124).

Should the heart line end in this area, devotion and dedication to the higher ideals of love are indicated.

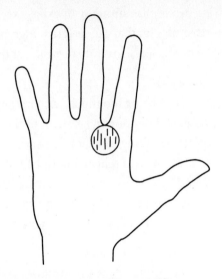

Figure 123: Mount one crossed by vertical lines

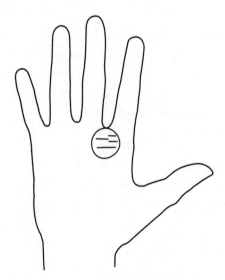

Figure 124: Mount one crossed by horizontal lines

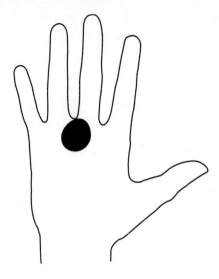

Figure 125: Mount two

Mount Two:
Saturn/Apollo
(see Figure 125)

Is the mount . . .

Well-developed, firm, and high?
A sign that the subject has good powers of logical thought and proceeds steadily toward goals, with an ability to complete things.

It can also show a desire for knowledge, religious tendencies, and prudence. The subject is likely to have leadership qualities, powers to inspire trust in others, and a great deal of patience.

A mount of this kind can be a measure of financial success—some traditions call it the money bump.

Overdeveloped?
A rare sign, it indicates how the qualities of intelligence and leadership may be devoted to bigotry and even tyranny. This could be a person who is domineering, selfish, and devoted to material gain no matter what the expense is to others.

Undeveloped, flat, or hollow?
Here there is the likelihood of a pessimistic outlook in this subject, giving rise to negative circumstances that seem to confirm their defeatist attitude, creating a vicious circle.

The challenge for this subject is to refuse to be negative, to come to grips with given tasks, and to carry them through with a determined, positive attitude, overcoming any lack of commitment or effort.

Crossed by vertical lines?
An indication of positive energy and effort that can in turn promote favorable circumstances.

If the fate line ends in this area, vital energy that will last long into old age is suggested (see Figure 126).

Crossed by horizontal lines?
These are stress marks and are a symptom of frustration or other problems in business or artistic life (see Figure 127).

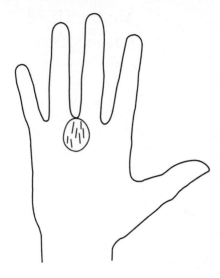

Figure 126: Mount two crossed by vertical lines

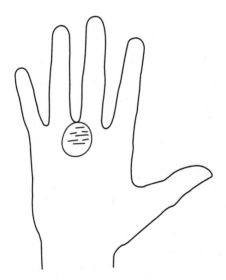

Figure 127: Mount two crossed by horizontal lines

Mount Three:
Apollo/Mercury
(see Figure 128)

Is the mount . . .

Well-developed, firm, and high?

This is a sign of positive feminine qualities corresponding to the yin principle and the anima.

This person will be compliant, flexible, and creative, with a cheerfully optimistic and generally accepting attitude.

A good balance between artistic and practical talents is also indicated.

Overdeveloped?

Signals exaggerated and distorted feminine qualities, as well as negative communication qualities—either artful dishonesty or outright lying.

Undeveloped, flat, or hollow?

The subject may be obstinate and quite impatient with others, having poor communication skills. The challenge for these impractical folk is to develop business skills, to nurture sympathy with others, and to cultivate a sense of good taste.

Crossed by vertical lines?

These are positive energy lines, representing artistic striving and the ability to overcome difficulties (see Figure 129).

If the sun line ends here, it is a sign that artistic activity continues well into old age.

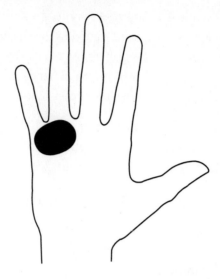

Figure 128: Mount three

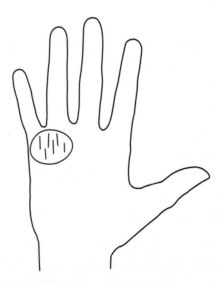

Figure 129: Mount three crossed by vertical lines

The medical stigmata may be present (see page 183). This sign is a major indication of the "healing hand" in the folk sense, indicating an ability to alleviate pain or distress by massage or other laying on of hands. It can also indicate an aptitude for the healing professions.

Crossed by horizontal lines?
These are stress marks indicating difficulties in the fields of work, communication, or the arts (see Figure 130).

Mount Four:
Mars Positive
(see Figure 131)

Is the mount . . .
Well-developed, firm, and high?
This mount represents the libido, the erotic and aggressive drive—the power of arousal and emotional vitality.

The strength or weakness of this mount affects all other aspects of the hand. It represents courage, self-control, and the ability to cope with emergencies.

A high degree of sexuality and strong sexual needs are also indicated.

Overdeveloped?
A sign of aggression and high levels of sexual energy.

If extreme, this can be an indication of anger and tyranny; a bully, aggressive in all areas of life.

Undeveloped, flat, or hollow?
Signifies low energy levels, a subdued and nonaggressive libido; possibly a timid and withdrawn character, a natural hermit.

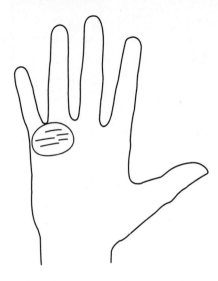

Figure 130: Mount three crossed by horizontal lines

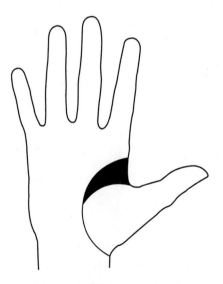

Figure 131: Mount four

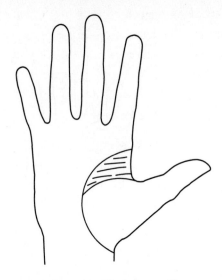

Figure 132: Mount four crossed by horizontal lines

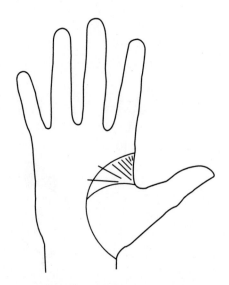

Figure 133: Mount four crossed by diagonal lines

Crossed by horizontal lines?

These are influence lines, representing the influence in early life of the subject's immediate family, and may be positive or negative. If negative, a confusion of lines—with islands, crosses, etc.—will appear on the life line at the point of contact (see Figure 132).

Crossed by vertical or diagonal lines?

These are stress lines, indicating problems in the area of childhood development, that affect the entire hand and the subject's life (see Figure 133).

Mount Five:
Mars Negative
(see Figure 134)

Is the mount . . .

Well-developed, firm, and high?

This is a measure of the strength of a person's animal spirits and capacity to enjoy day-to-day life.

It shows that the subject takes pleasure in sex and procreation and has a love of relationships and domestic life. He or she enjoys food and drink, and physical activity.

Overdeveloped?

This personality is governed by our animal (purely physical) spirits, which leads to a propensity for natural indulgence in sensuality and self-indulgence in food, sex, and other physical pleasures.

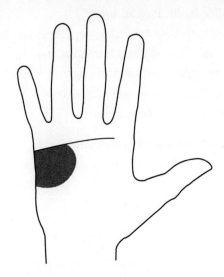

Figure 134: Mount five (with heart line)

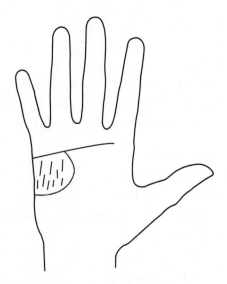

Figure 135: Mount five crossed by vertical lines

Undeveloped, flat, or hollow?

A sign of subdued or low physical energy, reflecting a person who takes little pleasure in domestic life or physical activity. They may be devoted to intellectual ideals and pursuits, and so seem cool and unresponsive to more robust people.

Crossed by vertical lines?

Verticals are always associated with positive energy. This is a person who devotes much effort to family, and whose life is rich and full of enjoyment. He or she probably regards having a good time as one of the more important considerations in life (see Figure 135).

Crossed by horizontal lines?

Signifies restlessness and stress in the area of life most affected by the animal spirits: family, courtship, pleasure, and physical activity.

Tradition has it that this indicates travel (see Figure 136).

Mount Six:
Venus
(see Figure 137)

Is the mount . . .

Well-developed, firm, and high?

Ruled by Venus, this mount represents the conscious emotional quarter of the personality, and is the largest mount. It denotes a cheerful, optimistic personality—warm, generous, sympathetic, sociable, and hospitable—with the capacity to enjoy life day to day.

This person is affectionate and attractive, sexual and physical, and emotionally stable.

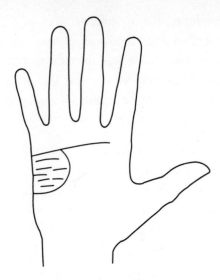

Figure 136: Mount five crossed by horizontal lines

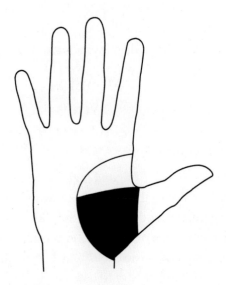

Figure 137: Mount six

Overdeveloped?

This is a very emotional and physical person who takes great pleasure in physical relationships and sex.

Their challenge is to avoid excess sensuality, inconstancy, vanity, and hedonism. The subject also needs to be aware that their heightened emotional responsiveness can become aggression.

Undeveloped, flat, or hollow?

A sign of repressed emotions, leading to apparent coolness and inhibition in the expression of love and affection. Sometimes egocentric and insensitive to others' needs, they are pragmatic rather than enthusiastic, frugal, and conservative. Their challenge is to be more sensitive and to express their emotions more, taking the initiative more often.

Crossed by vertical lines?

A sign of vitality and emotional energy, intense emotional and physical feelings, and the possibility of oversensitivity. This person has a love of life, relationships, and family. Each line can also represent the assistance given by another in a close, supporting relationship, such as a spouse.

People with many verticals usually have a lust for freedom, and may have an interest in self-development (see Figure 138).

Crossed by horizontal lines?

These are stress marks that may indicate interference or influence by other people, especially in sexual and family relationships (see Figure 139).

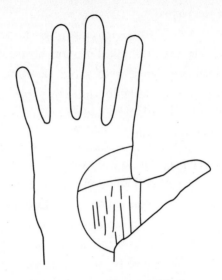

Figure 138: Mount six crossed by vertical lines

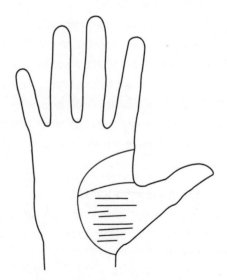

Figure 139: Mount six crossed by horizontal lines

Mount Seven:
Neptune
(see Figure 140)

Is the mount . . .

Well-developed, firm, and high?

This mount forms a bridge between the conscious mind and the instinctive, bio-automatic, subconscious self. It shows that good interaction between the left and right brain exists. People with this characteristic are compassionate and have a strong sense of self, the ability to communicate well on most levels, and an instinct for making correct decisions in most situations.

Overdeveloped?

The sign of an overactive imagination: one who may have difficulty distinguishing between reality and fantasy.

This person may also be self-centered and domineering.

Undeveloped, flat, or hollow?

This is a mark of people who are not in touch with their deeper motivations. They are largely unaware of their sub-conscious desires and motives, which can lead to a sense of personal conflict and feelings of angst and dissatisfaction. Such people feel they should be doing *something*—only they don't know what. They might find it useful to learn how to meditate, so they can connect with their deeper levels.

Crossed by vertical lines?

A sign of positive energy. The fate line may begin on this mount, indicating there is a fixed path of life that will be followed from an early age.

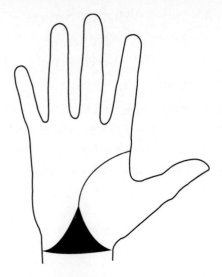

Figure 140: Mount seven

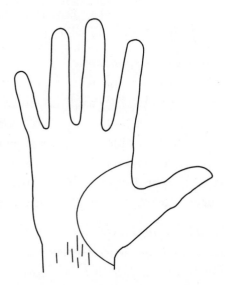

Figure 141: Mount seven crossed by vertical lines

Should the life line end here, a life of active mental and spiritual seeking is indicated, along with a strong likelihood of restlessness and wanderlust (see Figure 141).

Crossed by horizontal lines?
These are stress marks and show a proneness to addiction and dependency.

They also suggest strong sensual desires, and a tendency to overindulge (see Figure 142).

Mount Eight:
Lower Moon
(see Figure 143)

Is the mount . . .

Well-developed, firm, and high?
Denotes the existence of an active subconscious mind, and a high degree of spiritual development.

This person has a good sense of imagination, is refined, and has a talent for, or love of, poetry and music. He or she is attracted to change and travel.

Overdeveloped?
This is a sign of a very active subconscious mind and a high level of creativity. When badly aspected, it hints at a hyperactive imagination.

Undeveloped, flat, or hollow?
This sign represents the special challenge of the rigid authoritarian, who needs to overcome their inability to compromise and learn life-coping skills. They need to learn

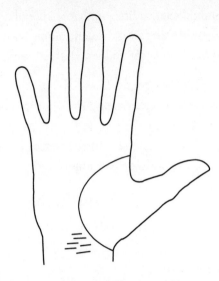

Figure 142: Mount seven crossed by horizontal lines

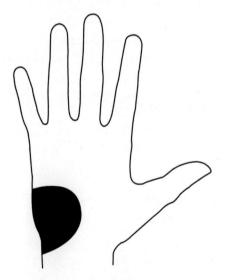

Figure 143: Mount eight

how to adapt to change. An inactive imagination and an indifference to others' feelings can be mitigated by conscious effort. The cultivation of meditation and a more spiritual outlook will also help.

Crossed by vertical lines?
Indicates high mental energy, with strong powers of imagination and visualization, and possible clairvoyance. Natural charisma is associated with this type of mount (see Figure 144).

The line of intuition usually begins in this area.

Crossed by horizontal lines?
Signifies a loss of self-control and of a sense of reality.

If there is one straight, long line, the subject may be prone to addiction and dependence, with strong sensual desires and a tendency to overindulge.

Some traditions say that these horizontals are indications of travel, particularly of journeys overseas (see Figure 145).

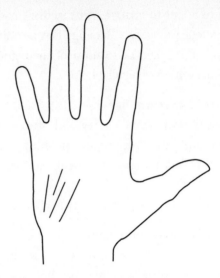

Figure 144: Mount eight crossed by vertical lines

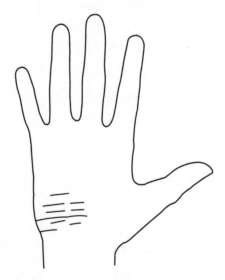

Figure 145: Mount eight crossed by horizontal lines

Further Details

These further details are subtleties that enhance and deepen the exploration of the character of the subject. Examine the fingers of the subject when he or she is in a relaxed attitude.

Fingers

Is there a space between . . .

Fingers one and two?

A mark of courage and an ability to face challenges. A generally dominant character, with good executive skills, who is self-sufficient, independent, and intolerant of the foibles of others (see Figure 146).

Fingers two and three?

A sign of ambition and the desire to be seen as dominant or charismatic. People with this characteristic often have difficulty working with others and making friends. Their challenge is to develop the habit of forethought and not to

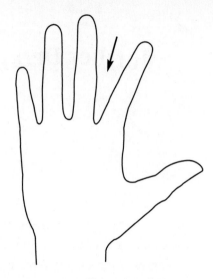

Figure 146: Space between fingers one and two

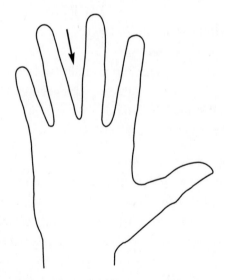

Figure 147: Space between fingers two and three

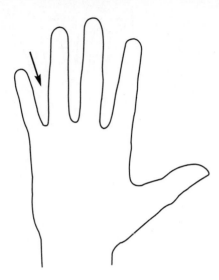

Figure 148: Space between fingers three and four

live day to day so much, and learn how to trust the motivations of others, despite their lack of trust in themselves (see Figure 147).

Fingers three and four?
An indication of someone in need of independence and privacy, who won't run with the herd.

This person prefers his or her own company to that of others, and may be uncommitted in relationships.

Sexual and emotional immaturity, or social isolation, are possible indications (see Figure 148).

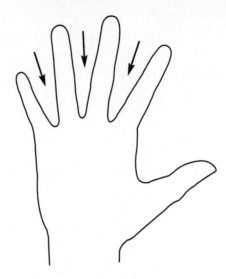

Figure 149: Space between all the fingers

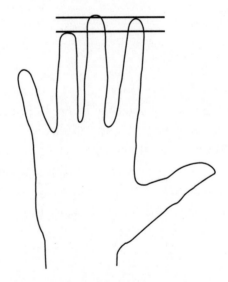

*Figure 150: Comparing the lengths of
fingers one and three*

All the fingers?

An extrovert; gregarious, confident, and probably self-sufficient. This person has good powers of self-expression, but is possibly intolerant of the views of others.

The traditional reading is of a headstrong personality (see Figure 149).

Look at the relative lengths of the fingers and their straightness. Is finger one longer than finger three?

Longer: Indicates a naturally dominant personality, with possible leadership skills and executive ability; one who likes to have their own way in most situations. Often considered bossy, this personality has difficulty obeying orders or directions (see Figure 150).

Shorter: A nondominant character—not weak but rather one who does not have a pathological need to be in control or command. Reasonably compliant and cooperative, this type is usually happy to let others take the lead.

Does finger one and/or two curve or bend toward finger three?

If so, it's a sign that the conscious intellectual energies lean toward the subconscious self. This person will generally allow his or her subconscious to make moral and practical decisions, i.e., the subject relies heavily on instinct, impulse, and hunches in making decisions.

The traditional meaning is of an instinctive knowledge of right and wrong (see Figure 151).

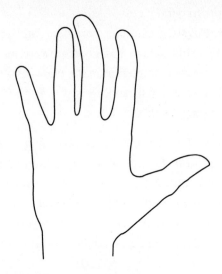

Figure 151: Fingers one and two
bending toward finger three

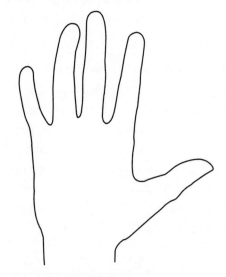

Figure 152: Fingers three and four
bending toward finger two

Does finger three and/or four curve or bend toward finger two?

If so, it's an indication that the subject's subconscious creative energies are striving for expression—that he or she has an active subconscious.

This person may be either a visionary or a dreamer, and may have an awareness of the invisible world of undefinable phenomena (see Figure 152).

Now, observe the fingers held in a relaxed attitude to notice if any of them cling together.

Do fingers one and two cling together?

This denotes powers of leadership; however, the capacity to initiate action is hampered by an acute lack of self-confidence (see Figure 153).

Do fingers two and three cling together?

This is an indication of self-abnegation and/or self-sacrifice, possibly due to the failure or frustration of dreams and ideals.

It can also mean repression: an artist forced to abandon the creative life, or a disillusioned romantic. Material and personal security may be a paramount consideration to the person with this characteristic (see Figure 154).

Do fingers one, two, and three cling together?

This is a sign of dependence upon others. This feature characterizes those in need of constant reassurance. They are sensitive to environmental influences and the surrounding atmosphere generally, and work well as team members.

✶

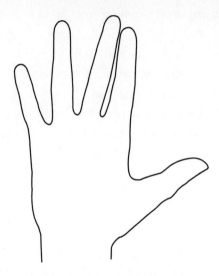

Figure 153: Fingers one and two clinging together

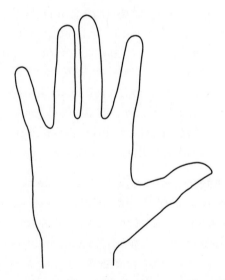

Figure 154: Fingers two and three clinging together

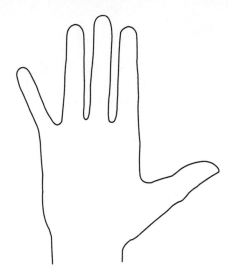

Figure 155: Fingers one, two, and three clinging together

They may have difficulties in expressing deeply personal ideas and feelings (see Figure 155).

Do fingers three and four cling together?
This shows ambition and desire for leadership and personal power without the necessary ability for achievement.

This person wishes to lead and inspire, but is without the substance or inner resources to do so at the present time (see Figure 156).

Do fingers two, three, and four cling together?
Indicates an ambitious person who is nevertheless lacking in aggressive drive; one who is likely to expend energy in areas where the competitive sense and aggression are not necessary for success (see Figure 157).

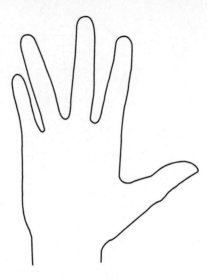

Figure 156: Fingers three and four clinging together

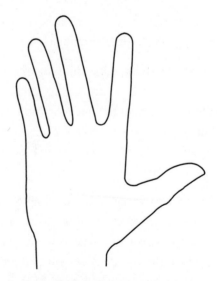

*Figure 157: Fingers two, three,
and four clinging together*

Figure 158: Whorl

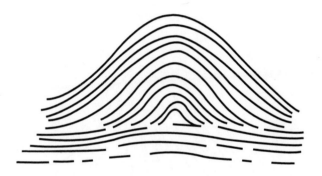

Figure 159: Arch

Examine the pattern of the fingerprints on the tip of each finger and the thumb. Use a magnifying glass if you wish. There are four main patterns.

Whorl (see Figure 158)

Arch (see Figure 159)

Loop (see Figure 160)

Tented Arch (see Figure 161)

Figure 160: Loop

Figure 161: Tented arch

Any pattern that does not fall into these forms, or is a combination of two or more of these forms, is a *composite*.

Is the pattern on finger one . . .

A whorl?
A sign of individuality; a creative, active, unique character with leadership qualities and a dislike of publicity. People with this pattern cling to their own views dogmatically and must be asked, not ordered.

A loop?
A charming, adaptable, and thoughtful leader, who can nevertheless be most practical.

An arch?
Signifies a person entrenched in his or her own personal viewpoint, with possibly fanatic views. However, this person can be realistic when it is for his or her own benefit.

A tented arch?
A sign of joie de vivre; an enthusiastic, youthful outlook.

A composite?
This is the mark of one who is more cautious and careful than versatile and adaptable.

Is the pattern on finger two . . .

A whorl?
Indicates a dislike of routine; one who is analytical, skeptical, self-exploring, and determined. This self-sufficient, self-protective person may be hard to sway from his or her own viewpoint.

A loop?
Practical, yet philosophical, this is the mark of one who is open-minded, honest, with a dislike of bias in others.

An arch?
Enjoyment and enthusiasm for work. Lack of an inner life, and inhibited. May avoid discussion of ideals.

A tented arch?
Idealistic, impractical. Caught up in speculation and philosophy.

A composite?
A person who is basically very practical and pragmatic.

Is the pattern on finger three . . .

A whorl?
A sign of creativity, artistic ability, and unconventional attitudes, this is nevertheless a self-controlled person whose feelings are based on well-defined and set patterns.

A loop?
Signifies craftsmanship, emotional and artistic freedom; an emotionally oriented, fashionable type.

An arch?
Indicates a love of science, precision, and machinery; possibly emotionally inarticulate, though, this person can be obsessive.

A tented arch?
Emotional, highly strung, and artistic, this may indicate one who has musical talent, personal flair, and is enthusiastic but impractical.

A composite?
Utilitarian and philistine attitudes.

Is the pattern on finger four . . .
A whorl?
This is the sign of a rugged individualist who carefully selects everything in life with an eye to interest and pleasure. Hedonistic, charming, and persuasive, this person is hard to influence.

A loop?
Indicates one who easily assimilates new ideas. Tactful and with good verbal skills, this person is a talker rather than a doer.

An arch?
This person is a primitive survivalist, with a low level of communication skills.

A tented arch?
Indicates a flair for learning languages.

A composite?
A sign of undeveloped language and communication skills.

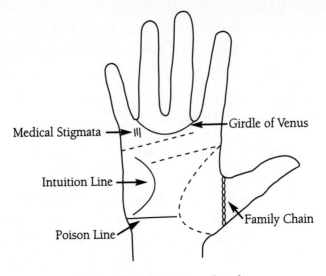

Figure 162: Minor lines on the palm

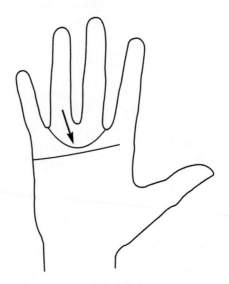

Figure 163: The girdle of Venus

Is the pattern on the thumb . . .

A whorl?
Indicates an individualistic and original character, with a strong will and a persevering nature.

A loop?
A practical, direct, deft, flexible person, with a diplomatic nature. May have a love of risk-taking.

An arch?
One who exhibits signs of indecision, suspicion, and caution, yet who has practical coping skills.

A tented arch?
A person with a flexible nature, who works and cooperates well with others, is charming, and has a tractable will.

A composite?
A sign of uncertainty; a slow-moving and thinking person, but generally quite enduring and persevering.

Now, examine the palm for the minor lines shown in the following illustration (see Figure 162).

The Girdle of Venus
Is the girdle of Venus clear and well-defined?
This is a sign of emotional hypersensitivity and sensuality belonging to restless personalities in need of continuous (and sometimes artificial) emotional stimulation. He or she may be prone to extreme mood swings and possess a naturally dependent nature, with a danger of addiction and dependency (see Figure 163).

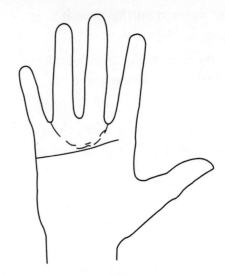

Figure 164: A broken girdle of Venus

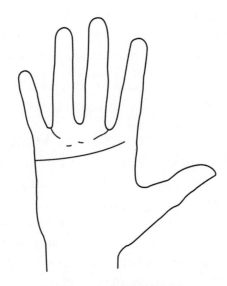

Figure 165: A fragmented girdle of Venus

Broken in one or more places?
Signifies emotional hypersensitivity and difficulties in achieving peace of mind and emotional fulfillment (see Figure 164).

Very fragmented; only partially present?
This shows a certain degree of emotional hypersensitivity—a person easily moved and very emotional in outlook and action (see Figure 165).

Medical Stigmata
Are the medical stigmata present?
The sign of a healer, these indicate an aptitude for medical or healing professions.

They are also called the Samaritan lines, and may indicate an ability to alleviate pain and discomfort by massage, laying on of hands, etc., or one with a healing personality (see Figure 166).

Intuition Line
Is the intuition line present?
In a water or fire hand, this is a sign of psychic ability and clairvoyance.

In earth and air hands, this is a positive indication of an active and guiding intuition and instinct; a natural sixth sense (see Figure 167).

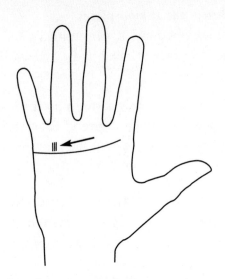

Figure 166: The medical stigmata

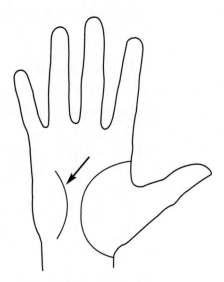

Figure 167: The intuition line

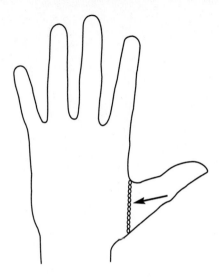

Figure 168: The family chain

The Family Chain
Is the family chain present?
This is said to indicate close family ties, and probably relates to dependence on family support and comfort.

This is the mark of one who functions best in the outside world from within the framework of a warm, tight family circle (see Figure 168).

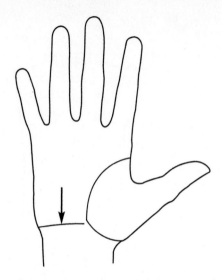

Figure 169: The poison line, or via lascivia

The Poison Line

Is the poison line present?

This is an indication of actual or potential dependency on drugs; a strong tendency to physical, emotional, and mental addiction.

Traditionally called the via lascivia, it was supposed to indicate a tendency to overindulgence.

It can also indicate presence of some type of allergy (see Figure 169).

Nails

The condition and shape of the nails show personality characteristics and general health. Many common problems with nails, such as softness, splitting, white spots, and so forth, derive from some form of malnutrition.

Are the nails . . .

Bitten?

Bitten nails are generally more than just a bad habit: they are a sign of stress, which can indicate poor emotional balance, general irritability, intolerance, introspection, and loneliness.

Bitten nails may indicate that the subject is not coping or adjusting well to aspects of his or her life.

Wider than they are long (short nails)?

This is the sign of people with a very critical, logical, and analytical approach to things. Often belligerent, argumentative, and stubborn, they may have an unforgiving streak in their character and be self-righteous and narrow-minded.

If the nail is very wide, the subject may also be bad-tempered, aggressive, and intolerant. It can also indicate a tendency to heart troubles.

Longer than they are wide (long nails)?
The sign of an intuitive, artistic, idealistic, and easygoing person who may lack physical energy and tend to ignore unpleasant facts or events. They can be ironic and sarcastic, but are generally peace-loving and slow to anger.

This may also show a tendency to chest and lung complaints.

Wedge-shaped (narrow at the base, widening at the top)?
A sign of anxiety; a person with poor nerves, and a disposition to worry. A tendency toward nervous or mental exhaustion is also indicated.

Oval-shaped?
A sign of a courteous, refined, sweet, and obliging nature—devoted and loyal. Honest, placid, and generally peaceful, people with this feature are nevertheless prone to overly emotional outbursts when stressed.

Very long and narrow (like talons)?
The mark of people with selfish natures and little regard for others. Grasping and greedy, they are often very persistent in the pursuit of their alms. It can also indicate malnutrition.

Do the nails . . .

Have moons?

With moons: This is a sign of a good physical constitution and a contented mind. If the moon has a bluish halo, it can be a sign of vascular problems, and may be an early warning of a stroke.

Without moons: According to tradition, this indicates a poor physical constitution. Research is needed here.

Have vertical ridges?

Also called senile nails, these are very common in the elderly. They can be an indication of inherited rheumatism or arthritis, and are related to chronic stress and to Darier's disease (a genetic skin disorder).

People undergoing radiation treatment often develop these ridges.

Have white spots?

These are an indication of calcium deficiency. They may also indicate fatigue, tension, or malfunction of the liver. Tradition tells us that white spots are symptomatic of unfortunate love affairs.

Now, note the color. Is the nail . . .

Red?

Hypertension; high blood pressure.

Pink?

Normal; indicates good health.

Blue?

Circulatory problems. If blue appears in the nails of one hand only, it can be an early warning of a stroke.

Very pale and colorless?

Poor diet, malnutrition, acute symptom of shock. It may also indicate cirrhosis of the liver or kidney problems.

Part Three
The Appendices

General Notes

Note for Astrologers

The connection of palmistry with astrology is obvious from the terminology they both use. They are similar in that they both attempt to create accurate, working analyses of people. Astrologers may use palmistry to confirm or clarify their own diagnoses. Certainly, many palmists use astrology to clear up points of palmistry.

For astrologers, palmistry can be a practical way to determine the strengths of aspects when they are ambiguous or obscure. A glance at the subject's hand will reveal the extent of the influence of any given planet (see Figure 170).

As it is interpretation, rather than mathematics, that lies at the base of the art of astrology, this cross-referencing, diagnostic tool may be valuable as clarification or confirmation.

See the diagram on page 194 for the astrological correspondences with the hand. The three phalanges of the four fingers give us the traditional twelve signs of the zodiac. The

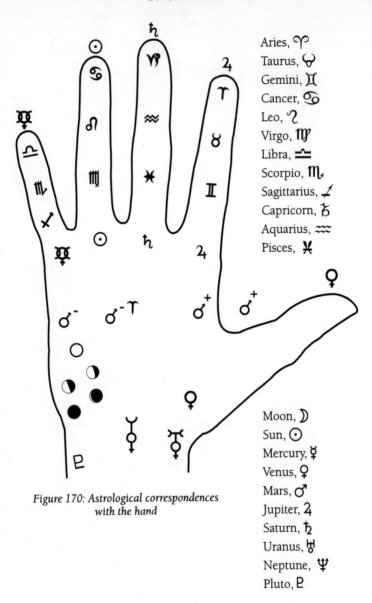

Aries, ♈
Taurus, ♉
Gemini, ♊
Cancer, ♋
Leo, ♌
Virgo, ♍
Libra, ♎
Scorpio, ♏
Sagittarius, ♐
Capricorn, ♑
Aquarius, ♒
Pisces, ♓

*Figure 170: Astrological correspondences
with the hand*

Moon, ☽
Sun, ☉
Mercury, ☿
Venus, ♀
Mars, ♂
Jupiter, ♃
Saturn, ♄
Uranus, ♅
Neptune, ♆
Pluto, ♇

★

thumb signifies the ego, and is called by some traditions the finger of Venus. It is the thumb, with its opposing grip to the fingers, that has allowed us to make so much technological progression. Without it, the use of tools would be impossible.

On the phalanges, there are four major marks to look for.

Verticals: these represent positive energy

Horizontals: these are bars and blocks of energy

Grilles: these indicate a scrambling of energy

Crosses: these signal that energy is being sidetracked

In astrological terms, a vertical would be a good aspect, horizontals would be a retrograde sign, a grille possibly neutral, and a cross a bad aspect.

Notice that planets and other astrological terms are used to describe the various mounts on the hand—the mount of Venus and the moon, for instance. This is a reflection of the old esoteric saying "As above, so below"— the fact that humans are the microcosm, the mirror of the greater cosmos.

The Role of Reflexology

The principles of reflex massage have been known and used for centuries, particularly in China. These principles were rediscovered by Doctor William Fitzgerald in 1913, and introduced into Western medicine as zone therapy. However, it has not been well accepted by mainstream medicine.

Reflexology is based on a similar theory to that of acupuncture: i.e., that the body has a vital life force that circulates along pathways encompassing the entire body. These pathways have been extensively documented by Chinese medicine, but they do not match with the nervous, circulatory, lymphatic, or any other system that Western medicine has so far been able to detect.

The pathways nevertheless exist, and their existence constitutes one of the major points of difference between the Western and Chinese theories of medicine.

These pathways can be tapped at more than 800 points on the body. The hands and feet, in particular, are rich in reflex buttons, which connect to all the major glands and organs. When these buttons or points are massaged or otherwise stimulated, they have a direct effect on the connecting organ. The stimulation of the points seems to have the effect of clearing the pathways so that the life energy can flow freely. (In Chinese theory, disease is often the result of blockages in the free flow of life energy through the channels.) The removal or easing of blockages assists the body to heal by allowing the normal healing processes to act without hindrance.

Regular massage can assist in alleviating and relieving both chronic and acute conditions. It can even be self-administered. One should not underestimate the healing aspects of simply holding and gently massaging someone's hand.

A properly conducted examination of a hand by a student of palmistry can constitute a reflexology massage. As you feel and squeeze the hands, seeking out the hollows (weaknesses) and testing the bulges (strengths), a feeling of relaxation and well-being in the subject should become evident. This is useful, as a palm reading can be a mild crisis for some people, provoking anxiety. They might be afraid that you will find some terrible doom to sour their future. In any case, the offering of the hands, palms up, is an attitude of submission and surrender, which in itself could make the subject feel vulnerable.

If you happen to locate any tender or painful spots, advise the subject to massage these points themselves later, as they probably represent some physical problem present in the body.

A full reflexology massage is a loving and healing gift to give anyone. Use a light oil and sit facing the subject as though for a palm reading. You must work each hand in turn, completing each step on both hands before moving on to the next step. Here are the steps:

1. Work your thumbs over each palm in a firm, circular motion.

2. Work the hollows between the tendons on the back of the hands. These are rich in acupressure points, and open the whole hand. Work from the wrist toward the fingers.

3. Massage the webbing between the fingers. These are considered toxic points, where tension may accumulate.

4. Now, take each finger in turn (including the thumb) and
    (a) tug it firmly,
    (b) gently twist it back and forth,
    (c) press hard on the tip,
    (d) work the spaces between the joints, concentrating on the sides of the fingers.

5. Lace your fingers with the subject's and stretch the fingers backward.

6. Stretch the thumbs back (but don't force them) toward the wrist several times.

7. Flex and fold the palm in on itself, using pressure on the sides of the hand.

8. Have the subject flap and wave the hands about in a loosening motion.

9. Use your fist to press all over the palm, then pound it gently, using the right fist and supporting with the left.

10. Give a brisk all-over rub.

Use this as a basic technique and do not hesitate to add your own variations. A great deal of variety is possible. Just do what feels right and loving.

Note for Parents

Palmistry is an excellent way to evaluate and understand your child's character. From the moment of birth, a wealth of information can be gleaned from your baby's hand. The three major lines are immediately present in the hands of babies. This shows that the three basic energies of the human animal are present—physical, emotional, and intellectual.

The hand of a child is very changeable. It can be interesting to take regular prints (or photocopies) of a growing hand and see how the lines and mounts reflect the emerging personality.

Changes in the lines can be dramatic: the emotional turmoil of puberty often creates much disruption in the form of islands and dots on the head and heart lines. Even more interesting, the early segments of the major lines will reflect your influence as a parent on the child.

The greatest benefit is, of course, your own increased perception and appreciation of your child's character. Their talents, intelligence, and faults can all be detected and evaluated from an early age. The sensitive, artistic child can be appropriately nurtured and encouraged; the intelligent or creative child can be given direction; and the high-energy, sports-minded type can be offered suitable outlets for that energy.

A general check on health can also be maintained by palmistry. Keep an eye out for stress marks on fingers during crucial periods such as examinations, starting new schools, and so on.

A sensitive familiarity with your children's hands (not to mention your spouse's) will assist both them and yourself.

Note for Personnel Managers

The task of the personnel manager might be fairly and simply stated as finding the right person for the right job. In the past twenty years a great number of psychological tests have developed to test job applicants for qualities such as leadership, math skills, motivation, intelligence, and much else.

The validity of many tests is often questionable. It is always possible to fake answers and manipulate results. Whatever the case, there are weaknesses inherent in many of the assumptions made by such tests. References are only partially helpful in assessing a candidate for a position, and often tell little of enduring traits of the potential employee. Many people are excellent at interviews, yet turn out to perform poorly on the job. Then again, someone who may be ideal for a position could be nervous at interviews and fail to impress.

Employers sometimes refer potential workers to graphologists, and others turn to astrologers. These methods are both useful—graphology in particular—but the majority of appointments seem to occur on the basis of references and tests.

As the hand is an unbiased map of one's abilities, talents, and potential, modern palmistry would be an ideal tool for assessing these characteristics. Desired and undesired qualities can be detected at a glance, with no possibility of deception. The palm cannot lie.

Are you looking for a manager? If so, the applicant's hand will tell you if the requisite qualities—organizational skill, honesty, reliability—are there. Are you seeking a supervisor with some creative flair, or one who is solid and capable of getting the job done as specified? Do you need a worker with a flair for figures, or one who is subtle and sensitive with clients? Is a worker honest? Is he or she ambitious, aggressive, happy to be in a subordinate position?

Palmistry can provide the answers to these decisions. For example, if you are seeking an executive, have a good look at the index finger (finger one). Is it longer than the ring finger (finger three)? If it is, you have a naturally dominant type who is unsuited by temperament to a subordinate position, especially where there is no scope for advancement. If the index finger is curved so that it leans toward the other fingers, it is a sign that the applicant has a problem with self-confidence, and doubts his or her ability.

Now look at the bottom phalange of the index finger. Is it strongly marked with vertical lines? If so, the person has good organizational skills and is capable of inspiring staff. If there are also bar lines or a grille, then there exists a strong tendency toward manipulation and perhaps a penchant for office politics, which may or may not suit you as an employer.

Now look at the head line. If it is clean, clear, and very straight, you have a logical type who will excel at figures, but may be poor at handling problems requiring sensitivity or creative flair. If you need an executive who is imaginative, sympathetic, and inventive, then look for a curved head line.

Does the job involve selling? Then look for strong vertical lines on the bottom phalange of the little finger (finger four). If there are bar lines in the area, you have a convincing liar before you.

Do you need a manager who is both practical and reliable, who will stick to the job stubbornly and single-mindedly? Then find an earth hand with a good head line and a strong fate line. Such a person can be counted on to be rather authoritative, though regrettably insensitive in the area of employer/employee relationships. He or she does not suffer fools gladly, and will have great difficulty understanding personal problems among the staff. On the other hand, a manager with a water hand would be ideal for positions requiring tact and sensitivity.

Positions requiring flexibility, enthusiasm, and good staff motivational skills would best suit the fire hand, while the job needing an analytical, systematic approach would best be filled by an air hand.

Using such simple guidelines, palmistry can be a useful cross-reference to established procedures, an alternative method of avoiding the costly misplacement of round pegs in square holes.

Note for Lovers and
Marriage Guidance Counselors

The gentle application of palmistry to the area of emotional relationships can greatly aid understanding between the parties involved. The exploration of character through the palm will help people to understand themselves and their partner, and areas of conflict and compatibility can be thoroughly explored.

In the palm, you will easily discover the really major differences that tend to cause conflict in relationships. Some are readily apparent: a strong sex drive versus a low sex drive, the security-conscious versus the rolling stone, the partygoer versus the stay-at-home type. Perhaps the partners are both dominant types, which can cause conflicts as each struggles to settle a pecking order.

There are many other differences, greater and lesser, that can escalate into disharmony and separation. You can also see how individual inner conflicts reflect in a relationship.

For the marriage guidance counselor, a mutual reading is a good idea: use a two-hour session, which can be formalized by such techniques as the use of a blackboard divided into three segments—two devoted to each individual, and one to their aspect as a couple. The idea is to list the main negative and positive qualities of each partner so that compatibilities and differences become obvious.

Each point should be discussed before committing it to writing. This segment of the session can be very lively due to palmistry's startling accuracy. This truthfulness is palmistry's great strength. Bluster and denial cease to be of much use when one is confronted with irrefutable truth.

Your attitude as a palmist is most important. You must be disinterested and objective, with no desire to sway anyone to any particular point of view, only to relate truthfully what you find in the hand.

The ability to accept the findings can be a measure of the subject's self-knowledge. A good guidance session is a direct confrontation with the truth. Individuals are brought face-to-face with their inner personalities, down to their deepest motivations.

The bottom line in fathoming human relationships is that love can only be based on mutual recognition and understanding.

However, it need not be too serious. Palmistry can be a party game or a lover's game, a voyage of mutual discovery, a way of sizing someone up before things get too serious. Such understanding can lead to the enhancement of a love match—or the opposite, an appreciation of why love cannot last. Either way, both parties will be better off.

The Esoterica

There are many systems of palmistry. The Indians and the Chinese, for instance, have systems that seem to be quite different from Western palmistry. There is evidence that the Egyptians and the Greeks also used palmistry.

The main thing all systems hold in common is the direct relationship between humanity and the cosmos. Since the hand is a map of the person, it could also be said that the hand is a map of the universe.

Each system of palmistry is based on varying cosmologies and belief systems. Take Indian palmistry as an example. It is probably trite to attempt to define the complexities and richness of Indian theology in just a few lines, but their philosophy tends toward theories of predestination: that people, driven by karma, lead fated lives. This idea of inevitability, from the New Age palmistry viewpoint, gives to Indian palmistry an unacceptable degree of insistence on future prediction.

Of course, the Indian system of palmistry works very well for Indians. It has evolved to fit their rigid caste system and their religiously defined social structure. In traditional rural villages the organization of the four major castes—the priests, the warriors, the merchants, and the untouchables—can be seen functioning today as it has for 2,000 years. It may be seen that the life of the individual is fated in such a rigid and stratified society. The sons of priests grow up to be priests and marry the daughters of priests. Marriage out of caste doesn't, as a rule, occur. Likewise, many occupations are inherited.

Social mobility is more common in Western society, and it is this that invalidates much of the Indian systems of palmistry for the New Age palmist. Cultural and philosophical differences also render some Chinese palmistry unsuitable, even though there are many points of similarity and correspondence.

Reflexology Chart

The illustration on page 208 attempts to display the relationship between the cosmos, represented by traditional astrological signs and meanings, and the microcosmos, each individual.

It shows the important division of the hand into four quarters: the conscious intellectual self, the subconscious intellectual self, the conscious emotional self, and the subconscious emotional self. It is possible to make a quick assessment of a subject simply by observing whether there is a concentration of marks or lines in any one quarter.

The strengths and weaknesses of a particular zone may be seen by noting the four common signs found in the palm: *verticals,* representing the positive flow of natural energy; *horizontals,* indicating stress and interruptions to the free flow of energy; *grilles,* which scramble and confuse energy; and *crosses,* which can either accentuate or divert energy.

Areas clear of markings signal positive potential energy.

The illustration is also useful as a psychological reflexology chart. Instead of showing the physical correspondences of areas of the hand, e.g., to heart, lungs etc., it shows the correspondences to the psychological aspects of a human being. These may be worked on with massage and affirmations, just as the physical aspects can be.

Psychological Reflexology Chart of the Human Hand

These zones show the relationships between the cosmos and microcosmos. The person's strengths and weaknesses in each zone may be discerned by seeking marks in any zone. There are five common signs:

Verticals: positive flow of natural energy

Bars: stress and breaks in flow of energy that confuse the flow of natural energy

Grilles: scrambles the flow of natural energy

Crosses: can accentuate or divert energy

Clear Area: positive potential energy (see Figure 171)

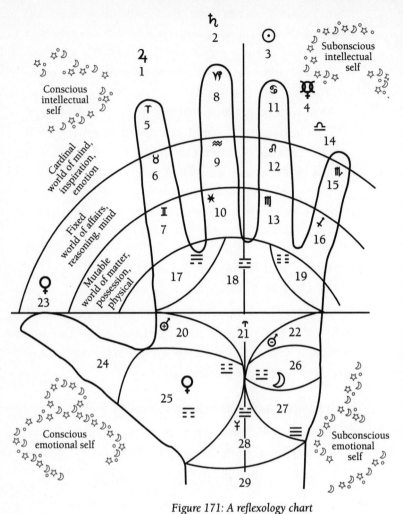

Figure 171: A reflexology chart

1—Jupiter finger: professional pride and ambition, vitality and power, leadership

2—Saturn finger: agriculture, invention, tradition and sentiment, seriousness and ritual

3—Sun finger: intelligence, art, boldness, coldness, creativity, humanity

4—Mercury finger: communication, intellect, precision, written and verbal skills, subtlety, outerness, wisdom

5—Aries (I Am), Fire, Active. Tarot: The Emperor. Inspiration, spiritual or religious fervor, executive skills, leadership versus officiousness

6—Taurus (I Have), Earth, Fixed. Tarot: High Priest, Pope. Determination and persistence, nobility, ethics, reliability, ambition, stability versus stubborness

7—Gemini (I Think), Air, Mutable. Tarot: The Lovers. Manipulation, versatility, plausibility, financial drive, versatility versus restlessness

8—Capricorn (I Use), Earth, Active. Tarot: The Devil. Sense of right and wrong, source of morality, honesy versus deceit

9—Aquarius (I Know), Air, Fixed. Tarot: The Star. Search for truth, academic or physical energy, altruism versus cupidity

10—Pisces (I Believe), Water, Mutable. Tarot: The Moon. A buffer against the world, propriety and comfort, sympathy versus paranoia

11—Cancer (I Feel), Water, Active. Tarot: The Charioteer. Extreme sensitivity, high creative skill, originality and energy

12—Leo (I Will), Fire, Fixed. Tarot: Strength. Expressiveness, talent, need to express creative energy, love versus domination

13—Virgo (I Analyze), Earth, Mutable. Tarot: The Hermit. Prudence, talent for commercial art, analysis and perception, analysis versus criticism

14—Libra (I Balance), Air, Active. Tarot: Justice. Communication to all, love of liberty, diplomacy, harmony, selfishness versus selflessness

15—Scorpio (I Desire), Water, Fixed. Tarot: Death. Personal communication, intimate, honesty, lust versus morality

16—Sagittarius (I See), Air, Mutable. Tarot: Temperance. Honesty, enthusiasm, frankness, loyalty versus promiscuity

17—Personal powers, pride, love of art and ritual, masculinity

18—Tradition, prudence, wealth, sentiment, sorrow, patience, resignation, temper, confidence

19—Skill, cleverness, business, communication, science

20—Sexuality, aggression, passion, reckless actions

21—Self-image, energy, enthusiasm

22—Passive resistence

23—Venus finger (The ego), will, energy, confidence, power, temper and stubborness

24—Reason, logic, individuality

25—Understanding, love, music, passion, emotion, attraction, stamina, joie de vivre

26—Courage, procreation, protection, calm, domesticity, pleasure, animal spirits

27—Refinement, spiritual development, intuition, personal development, prophecy, poetry, selfishness

28—Harmony and communication

29—Bridge between the conscious and bio-autimatic, instinctive mind

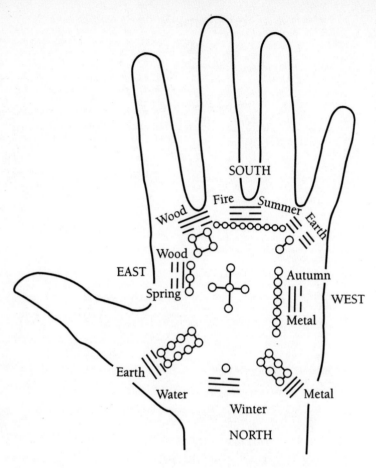

Figure 172: The eight mounts as defined by the I Ching

The Chinese Hand

This illustration is a symbolic graphic, derived from the I Ching, and rendered onto the hand.

Students of the I Ching may spend hours finding areas of intriguing correspondence with the traditional Western layouts of the hand. An interesting aspect is the number of points of agreement between the Oriental and Occidental systems for, despite the fact that they depart on most points, they ultimately come to very similar conclusions (see Figure 172).

Here is a brief list of the qualities of the eight mounts as defined by the I Ching.

Mount One (Jupiter/Saturn)
Wind, wood, southeast, the eldest daughter, the thigh, early summer, midmorning, flexibility, gentleness, and gradual, penetrating influence.

Mount Two (Saturn/Apollo)
Fire (sun, lightning), South, the middle daughter, the eye, midsummer, noon, brightness, elegance, intelligence, and illumination.

Mount Three (Apollo/Mercury)
Earth, Southwest, the mother, the belly, early autumn, night, capaciousness, submission, yielding, darkness, responsive, receptivity, and nourishment.

Mount Four (Mars positive)
Thunder, East, the eldest son, the foot, spring, early morning, arousal, activity, movement, and exciting power.

Mount Five (Mars negative/Upper Luna)

Water (a lake or a marsh), West, the youngest daughter, the mouth, late autumn, twilight, satisfaction, fullness, complacency, and pleasure.

Mount Six (Venus)

Mountain, Northeast, the youngest son, the hand, late winter, dawn, tranquillity, resting, being calm, patience, waiting, and immovability.

Mount Seven (Neptune)

Water (rain and clouds), North, the middle son, the ear, midwinter, midnight, difficulty, danger, and anxiety.

Mount Eight (Moon)

Heaven, East, the father, the head, early winter, daytime, creativity, strength, and untiring power.

The Traditional Hand

The following is a description of the ideal progression of a life, and is derived from a mediaeval manuscript.

Life is a cyclic process: all that exists goes through an inevitable cycle of birth, growth, maturity, decay, and death, and this is reflected in the hand.

From birth to puberty is our period of growth. During this time we are conditioned to the basic attitudes and values that shape our lives. Further growth occurs during our teen years (the age of reason), when further education takes place.

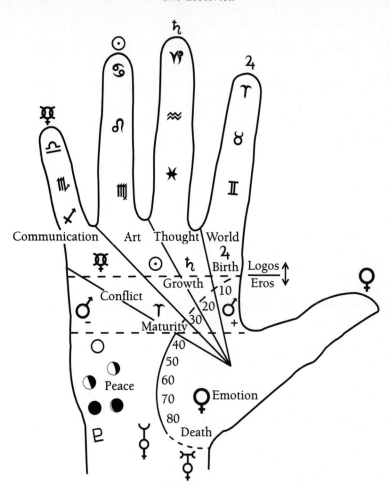

Figure 173: Traditional hand

Maturity comes as we begin to apply ourselves to the creation of a lifestyle. Acquired skills are practiced and perfected.

Gradually, growth ends and we are mature. The achievement of maturity should usher in a long period of peace and contentment. The ideal pattern for life is clear—birth, education, work, peace, and fulfillment.

Of course, the time spans of these processes vary greatly in each individual. Some people remain longer in one stage or another, while others move rapidly through the early stages of their development to arrive at fulfillment and peace. What stage are you in? (See Figure 173.)

The Wiccan Hand

The extremely ancient belief system known as Wicca divides the person into seven layers (or levels) inside two bodies (or forms). The seven layers relate to planets. The two forms represent the perishable personality and the imperishable (or eternal) part of the self.

The Perishable Persona

1: *Basal*
This is the entire hand, particularly the mount of the moon, and is symbolized by the Earth.

2: *Lower Astral*
This contains instinct, passion, and desire, and is symbolized by Mars.

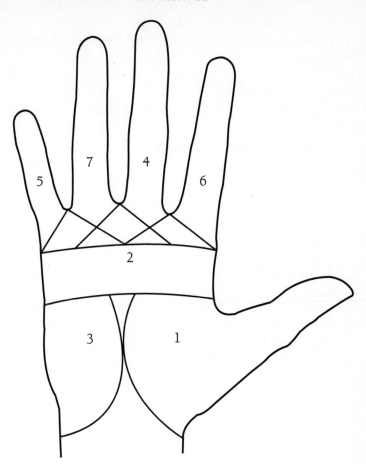

Figure 174: Wiccan hand

3: Upper Astral
This contains abstract emotion and idealism, and is ruled by Venus.

4: Lower Mental
This is the concrete mind, ruled by Saturn.

The Imperishable Persona

5: Upper Mental
Ruled by Mercury.

6: Upper Spiritual
Ruled by Jupiter.

7: Upper Spiritual
Ruled by the Sun (Apollo).

These three eternal areas represent creative power and energy (see Figure 174).

Further Reading

Brenner, Elizabeth. *The Hand Book* (1980), Bay Books, Sydney.

Cheiro, *Language of the Hand* (1967), Corgi, London.

Fitzherbert, Andrew. *Hand Psychology* (1986), Angus & Robertson, Sydney.

Germain, C. de Saint. *The Practice of Palmistry* (1973), Newcastle Publications, New York City.

St. Hill, Katherine. *Grammar of Palmistry* (1973), Sugar Publications, New Delhi.

West, Peter. *Lifelines* (1973), Piper Press, New Delhi.

Index